The Political Economy of Private Saving in the U.S.

The Political Economy of Private Saving in the U.S.

Evidence on the Social Opportunity Costs of Public Policy

Franklin G. Mixon, Jr., PhD
The University of Southern Mississippi
and
Kamal P. Upadhyaya, PhD
University of New Haven

Writers Club Press
San Jose New York Lincoln Shanghai

The Political Economy of Private Saving in the U.S.
Evidence on the Social Opportunity Costs of Public Policy

Writers Club Press
an imprint of iUniverse, Inc.

For information address:
iUniverse, Inc.
5220 S. 16th St., Suite 200
Lincoln, NE 68512
www.iuniverse.com

ISBN: 0-595-24548-X

Printed in the United States of America

About the Book

Using theoretical and empirical approaches from the economics and political science disciplines, this book examines the social opportunity costs of American public policy towards national saving. The primary focus of the text is on the institutional arrangements of the U.S. Social Security system, as they relate to Americans' decisions to save and invest, and to interest groups' decisions to lobby Congress for political privileges. The book presents statistical evidence suggesting that the social opportunity costs of U.S. policy in this area are enormous. Lower bound estimates put the loss in private savings, due to savers' decisions to substitute Social Security for private retirement plans, at approximately $349 billion dollars annually. When the lobbying costs associated with efforts to redistribute the money in the Social Security Trust Fund are included, this figure rises by perhaps as much as $15 billion. The results and discussion in this work should serve as a useful addition to the policy debates in this area.

Keynotes

Theoretical and empirical investigation of public policy towards national saving in the U.S.

The political economy of national saving in the U.S.

An economic analysis of the U.S. Social Security System.

A public choice approach to government policy towards national saving in the U.S.

A public choice study of Social Security and national saving in America.

Transfer seeking and the Social Security Trust Fund

Contents

Preface

We constructed this book to serve (mainly) as a contribution to the scholarly debate on public policy and its relation to national saving. We also hope that it might useful as a textbook supplement in a standard money and banking course, and/or a useful reading supplement for a public policy course in political science. Therefore, most of our readers will be academic researchers, economics/political science educators, and students of economics/political science. Perhaps we are overly ambitious, but we also hope we have written a book whose main points are at least partially accessible outside of these narrow circles listed above. We have probably come closer to this last goal in some places more than others.

In any event, we wish to thank (without implicating) many colleagues, friends, and professional associates who have generously given us their insights on many of the subjects covered in this book, either through personal conversations and anecdotes, conference presentations/discussions and correspondence, or through reading over drafts of our work at various stages in the process. This list of individuals includes Richard Ault, Alok Bohara, Brian Caldwell, Steve Caudill, Rohan Christie-David, John Cochrane, Mark Crain, Ronnie Davis, Mark Dickie, Bob Ekelund, Martin Feldstein, Thomas Garrett, Troy Gibson, David Hobson, Randall Holcombe, Yu Hsing, John Jackson, Ethel Jones, David Laband, Tom Lindley, Jody Lipford, Jim Long, John Lott, Russell McKenzie, Taisa Minto, Gyan Pradhan, Jeannie Raymond, Rand Ressler, Charles Rowley, Charles Sawyer, William Shughart, Russell Sobel, David Sollars, Frank Stephen, Thomas Stratmann, Dan Sutter, Jim Swofford, Mark Taylor,

Bob Tollison, Len Treviño, Gordon Tullock, Matt Tyrone, Keith Watson, Randall Wilder, James Wilkinson, and Jeffrey Wooldridge. We are also grateful to the late Mancur Olson for reading some of our earlier (related) research and offering his thoughtful advice. Many of the individuals listed above are our former teachers; some are our former students. In either case, we have both learned much from them.

Franklin G. Mixon, Jr.
Kamal P. Upadhyaya

August 2002

List of Tables

Chapter 1

Introduction and Background

On a recent visit to the Heritage Foundation's website (www.heritage.org/socialsecurity/), we took a minute to examine the Foundation's Social Security calculator. Like many of you, we have played this game before. We filled in the questionnaire as a 25 year old male. The computer assigned to us the average income for our gender/age ($28,872 per year), our life expectancy (77.61 years), and our legal retirement age (67 years) in terms of the Social Security laws. What came out, as always, was astonishing. Over his lifetime, this 25 year old male will contribute a total of $360,893 in payroll taxes, and, upon retirement at 67, receive a benefits payment of $2,391 per month. This results in an "investment" yielding a -0.72% per year return.

On the other hand, had this money been "invested" (economists prefer the term "saved") as a Personal Retirement Account—with 50% in stocks and 50% in U.S. Treasury bonds (i.e., a moderately conservative portfolio)—the $360,893 would have accumulated to $1,020,235 and the individual would have enjoyed an "investment" that yielded 4.89%. Additionally, unlike the Social Security System, this (now) 67 year old

1

male could receive the payment monthly or all at once, or even leave any remaining amount to his children, grandchildren or other heirs upon his death (at the age of 77.61). This is not an atypical scenario. Sure, when we change the individual's age and/or gender, the numbers shift a bit. But the conclusion found here is generally the same in any case. It is this conclusion that has also fueled the heated debate over reforming the U.S. Social Security System in the past few years.

This type of analysis/comparison is certainly interesting (and entertaining, if you can stand to think about it). Through website presentations of the sort at The Heritage Foundation, analyses such as this are also informing larger and broader audiences of the lagging results from the Social Security System in the United States. This is evident in survey polling suggesting that America's younger generations favor multiple private options over the current system.

What is not as widely known, however, is the degree to which important macroeconomic variables such as saving and investment are adversely affected by the U.S. Social Security System. Even less well known to Americans is the degree of lobbying effort—and its attendant social opportunity costs—surrounding access to money that flows into the Social Security Trust Fund each year from excess payroll tax receipts. This book addresses, both conceptually and empirically, these two problems surrounding our current federalized retirement system. Throughout the book we offer economic hypotheses from the public choice tradition that are supported by inference, anecdote and empirical evidence (usually in the form of data collection and regression analysis). As a preview, our work suggests that the lost savings and transfer seeking costs (i.e., lobbying costs) created by the current system have historically summed to as much as 3-percent (a conservative, lower bound estimate) of national income. This result is quite astonishing, and is explored in further detail here.

Chapter 2

Back to the Basics: The Dynamic Benefits from Private Saving

2.1. Introduction

Business and financial market events in America during the Spring and Summer of 2002 became a popular topic of conversation and discussion around workplace water coolers and household dinner tables, not to mention finance and other business school classrooms. Auditing and financial reporting scandals involving well-known business entities such as WorldCom and Enron have dominated nightly news reports, and the recent large swings in the Dow Jones Industrial Averages have caused some concerns among individual savers in the U.S. Over the past decade, Americans have become involved in U.S. and global equities markets at unprecedented rates, seeking higher returns than those often experienced from holding other financial instruments such as certificates of deposit and traditional passbook savings accounts. Though many individual savers are becoming increasingly concerned about market volatility, most financial historians and experts are quick to point out that current trends are much different than the disastrous scenarios of the past (e.g., 1930s, 1970s), where market volatility was usually accompanied by severe economic difficulties and/or other financial sector problems.

As Hubbard (2000: 2) points out, the "extensive media coverage of financial system events—prices of stocks and bonds, the health of banks [and corporations], what the Federal Reserve chairman did or didn't say—reflects the influence of money and the financial system on the U.S. economy and other economies around the world."[1] As Hubbard goes on to point out (2000: 2-3), financial "…markets react to the performance of the economy and the changes in fortunes of individual businesses, and changes in financial markets determine the rewards to savers and borrowers—and the ability of individuals to achieve wealth and prosperity." What we must understand to fully appreciate these ideas, as Hubbard suggests, is the basic roles of *money* and the *financial system* in our economy. This chapter will, following Hubbard, briefly examine some of these basic principles. These principles will develop a foundation for examining the general topic of this book—the social opportunity costs of public policy (in the U.S.) toward national (private) saving.

2.2. Money and the Financial System: A Brief Review of their Roles in the Macroeconomy

Any foray, however brief or extensive, into the subject of **money** and **financial systems** involves developing the argument for the important role each of these concepts plays in terms of specialization and trade, and economic growth and productivity. As Hubbard (2000) points out, money is an integral part of all modern economies:

"In economies of early stages of development, most individuals are self-sufficient. They grow their own food, build their own homes, and make their own clothes and tools. Such societies do not prosper greatly because, in doing everything, an individual does some tasks well and does others poorly. In more developed economies, individuals rely on **specialization**, producing the goods and services for which they have relatively the best ability. Individuals then *exchange*, or trade the goods or services they produce for those they need. If a furniture maker trades with a boat builder, they produce more and better furniture and boats than if each produced both with no exchange. Moreover, by encouraging production and higher-quality goods—and thus income—an economy's allowance for specialization and trade increases its citizens' standard of living. To reap the benefits of specialization, an economy must develop ways for individuals to exchange goods with one another. Then each person can obtain all the goods he or she needs, or wants, to consume." (Hubbard, 2000: 15)[2]

Most money and banking (and economics principles) texts compare three choices societies have used (historically) to exchange goods and services. These are barter, government allocation, and the use of money. Individuals can exchange goods/services by trading output directly with one another. This type of exchange is called barter. As children, we have all likely engaged in this activity (e.g., trading baseball cards, comic books, etc.), and it usually accomplished our desires quite well. For an economic system to function under this scheme is another story. As Hubbard (2000: 15) points out, first "effort must be spent searching for trading partners—a type of **transactions cost**, that is, the cost of trade or exchange. A second drawback is that each good has many prices." For instance, a furniture maker might be able to exchange eight chairs for three bushels of wheat, ten chairs for a boat, or a table for a wagon. "Needless to say, you would have to think hard about how to make informed decisions about which is the best" buy (Hubbard, 2000: 15-16). For instance, a barter economy with only 100 goods would have 4,950 prices, given that each good must be priced (as some ratio) in terms of each of the *other* goods in the market. Going further, an economy with 10,000 goods would utilize 49,995,000 prices (Hubbard, 2000: 16). These calculations are based on the formula for telling us how many prices we need when there are N goods in the economy (that is, Number of prices = $[N(N\text{-}1)]/2$). Economists sometimes refer to the costs associated with utilizing this large number of prices or exchange rates (associated with barter) as the **knowledge requirement**.[3]

There are at least three additional problems with barter: *standardization*, the *double coincidence of wants*, and *storage*. The first of these arises when we consider that for most goods, such as a furniture maker's chair and a farmer's sack of wheat, quality and/or size can vary substantially (Hubbard, 2000). The fourth drawback of barter is that each "individual must have exactly the good that the other [trading partner] wants for the exchange to take place—a situation economists call a *double coincidence of wants* (Hubbard, 2000: 16)." This problem would be evident in our lives quite often, given that we (the Authors) shop for food, medical care, transportation, and so on, and would mainly have lectures, articles and books to offer these merchants in return. We are not likely to find many willing trading partners, among the segments of the population that we usually encounter, in our quest for goods and services. Finally, "imagine the difficulty of storing value when goods are perishable [i.e., they cannot be saved]. Tomatoes are valuable in exchange only when they are fresh, for example (Hubbard, 2000: 16)." The problems associated with barter, along with government allocation, are summarized in Table 2.1.

Table 2.1

Summary of the Costs Associated with Barter and Government Allocation Schemes

---

Barter: when individuals exchange goods and services by trading output directly with others.

- **transactions costs**: effort spent searching for trading partners

- **knowledge requirement**: each good has many prices
- **standardization**: each good produced in different sizes, configurations, quality grades
- **double coincidence of wants**: each trading partner must have exactly what the other trading partner wants for exchange to take place
- **storage**: when goods are perishable, value cannot be stored

Government Allocation: a central authority collects the specialized output of each individual producer and distributes it to others according to some plan.

- **knowledge/information and coordination problems**: no concept of the value of (or demand for) goods, and information about the opportunity cost of production is lacking.
- **productive/allocative *inefficiencies***: Reduces incentives to be productive or cost efficient, and goods are not likely to flow to those who place the highest value on them (at least not at low cost).

Sources: Hubbard (2000) and the Authors.

As Hubbard (2000: 16) suggests, another option "is to sidestep voluntary trade and use **government allocation** to distribute goods and services. In this system, a central authority collects the specialized output of each individual producer and distributes it to others according to some plan." Perhaps the only advantage over barter that this system maintains is relative simplicity. However, as Hubbard (2000) points out, this system is not likely to prove useful in a changing economy given shifts in the costs of producing individual goods and services or shifts in the value that consumers place on different goods and services; in the latter case, goods are not likely to flow (in proper amounts) to those consumers who place the highest value on them (at least not at low cost). As Hubbard states,

"Ignoring market forces reduces incentives to produce and leaves consumers unhappy with the goods and services they receive (Hubbard, 2000: 16)." Under this scenario, one can envision long lines and very high opportunity costs associated with acquiring goods and services on a daily basis, assuming those goods are available in the first place. The lack of food in Cuba—a culture with a wonderful culinary tradition and some of the best cuisine available in the world—is clear evidence of the costs associated with this form of allocation. Then there are the millions of Eastern Europeans who, throughout the 20th Century, struggled with communism's inability to produce/allocate goods efficiently who can also attest to these costs. We don't even have to look far beyond our own situation on campus, where the perennial concern among students is the lack of parking space, and the distance from classrooms of most student parking spaces. Parking provision is typically a command decision made by a faculty/staff council, with modest student representation (i.e., Student Government Association officials, etc.). As a result, the "outnumbered" students receive parking allotments on the fringes of campus, while faculty/staff receive prime locations near the center of campus, despite the fact that many faculty are indifferent between driving and walking/bicycling to campus, while many students hold white-collar jobs and would pay a premium for parking. Currently, there is a debate on the campus at The University of Southern Mississippi about the fairness of Student Government officers receiving faculty parking permits (remember, the SGA was in on the process!).

After examining the costs associated with these two schemes, how can people benefit from specialization without incurring the high trading costs of barter or the inefficiencies (and "unfairness") of government allocation. "They can use **money**. Money eliminates the need for people to have a double coincidence of wants (Hubbard, 2000: 16)." It also reduces the knowledge requirement (i.e. a world with 100 goods will have 100 money prices), it is a value that can be stored, and it serves as a unit of account, or as a way of measuring value/costs in an economy. As Hutchinson (1992: 3) describes it:

> "To put the whole issue in a more positive vein, what are the social *merits* of money? In a phrase, an efficiently operating money system is a *sine qua non* for economic development and high living standards. It underlies and facilitates both specialization and capital formation—two essential ingredients of economic growth."

Thus, money offers a solution to the problems associated with the other two mechanisms. Next, we turn to a brief look at the role of the financial sector, in combination with money, in providing a higher standard of living for individuals and households.

According to Hubbard (2000: 4), the financial system is "a network of markets and institutions to bring savers and borrowers together."[4] The three groups of potential savers and borrowers in an economy are households, businesses, and governments. The financial system transfers savers' funds to borrowers and provides savers with payments for the use of their funds (i.e., interest payments). In the U.S. and other industrial economies, *private* networks in the financial system generally channel funds between savers and borrowers. These include, but are not limited to, commercial banks, savings and loan associations, credit unions, mutual savings banks, insurance companies, mutual fund companies, and pension fund companies. These *intermediaries* gather and communicate information about borrowers' circumstances so that individual savers do not have to search out prospective borrowers themselves. "In this way, the financial system allocates funds efficiently because it reduces the cost of information in matching savers with borrowers (Hubbard: 2000: 5)."

"Savers and borrowers use the financial system because each gets something in return: Borrowers can use savers' funds productively until savers themselves need the funds,…[and savers receive] three key **financial services**: risk sharing, liquidity, and information (Hubbard, 2000: 5)." It is the former part of this passage that we will emphasize—the fact that borrowers can use savers' funds "productively." As Hutchinson states:

> Capital formation, the process whereby new capital goods are produced,…depends heavily on a[n efficient] money [and financial] system. Fundamentally, capital formation requires saving to release productive resources from the production of consumer goods and transference of those released resources to the building of plants, equipment, and other capital goods."
> (Hutchinson, 1992: 3).

It is savers' funds (i.e., their unspent income) that are diverted from the purchase of consumer goods and, instead, saved. These savings are used by businesses to produce capital goods. It is, finally, the economy's *positive* response to this increased capital formation that forms the basis for the **social value** of money and an efficient financial sector. These concepts are summarized in the schematic presented below in Table 2.2.

Table 2.2
Money, the Financial Sector and Economic Growth: A Schematic Summary

Money→Specialization/Division of Labor→Higher Living Standards

Money & Efficient Financial System→Greater Saving→Capital Formation→Economic Growth

---

References: Hutchinson (1992); Hubbard (2000); the Authors.

There are numerous channels through which the ability of money and the financial system to efficiently transmit income from savers to investors can be hindered. For instance, inflation distorts the reward to saving, and can have an impact on the types of saving that will occur. In order to escape the effects of severe inflation, individuals may choose to hold non-financial assets (i.e., physical property, etc., instead of bank accounts, bonds, or stocks). Notice that this decision does not channel funds to investors; instead, surplus income units are used to purchase physical assets in the hope of avoiding the deterioration in purchasing power from a severe inflation. In this event, business enterprise lacks access to the funds that would support the capital formation that is necessary to provide greater rates of economic growth and higher living standards.

Economist Robert Barro, an expert on the factors related to economic growth and development, has examined inflation and growth data from a large panel of countries (Barro, 1999). As Barro's (1999: 98) research indicates (emphasis added):

> "In particular, the data would *not reject* the hypothesis that the *relation between growth and inflation is negative* at low rates of inflation and of the same magnitude as that for higher rates of inflation. Moreover, there is no sign in any range of a positive relation, which would suggest that higher inflation had to be tolerated to obtain more growth."

These results also support his finding of a *negative* and *significant* relationship between *inflation* and the level of *investment*, and thus *saving*, from the cross-country analysis (Barro, 1999: 34).

Inflation, like many other economic variables, is tied to public policy, institutions and government intervention. Many studies have pointed out that the institutional arrangements regarding a country's central bank have important consequences for inflation. Specifically, studies have suggested that the more politically independent a nation's central monetary authority, the lower the level of inflation in the country over time, *ceteris paribus* (Cukierman, 1992; Alesina and Summers, 1993).[5] These studies supplement others (see Havrilesky, 1995; Alesina, Roubini with Cohen, 1997) that point out the partisan effects in monetary policy, the political roots of government deficits/debt, and the harm that these phenomena can inflict on the macroeconomy. Studies such as these and others, therefore, build the groundwork for analyzing the negative effects of public policies and choices on important economic variables, such as national saving.

2.3. *Concluding Thoughts*

This chapter has built a framework for examining the socially beneficial role of saving in a macroeconomy. The social benefits, focusing solely on the production side of the coin, consist of having one's surplus income (i.e., one's savings) used "productively" for a time by businesses, which employ the funds to build up capital and equipment for future production. This capital formation, which flourishes in the presence of an efficient monetary system and financial markets, provides greater rates of economic growth and a higher standard of living. This chapter has also paved the way for analyzing the social costs of public policy toward saving, and thus investment and economic growth, in the macroeconomy. For much of the remainder of the book we examine a government policy and institutional arrangement—public retirement support through the U.S. Social Security system—that redirects otherwise *socially productive* saving effort toward consumption expenditures (Chapter 3). Following the exposition above, such an outcome would work to reduce aggregate investment and economic growth in the economy.

Notes to Chapter 2

1. R. Glenn Hubbard is the author of a popular textbook for university courses in money and banking (*Money, the financial system, and the economy*, Reading, MA: Addison-Wesley, copyright 2000, Third Edition). He is currently serving as chief economic advisor to President Bush. As a review for students, this chapter will make significant use of his text to define the importance of money and

financial markets in the economy. We will also rely (in part) on Hutchinson (1992).

2. As Hutchinson (1992: 3) puts it:

    "[Money] did not originate centuries ago with some far-sighted government that saw the need for money and responded by offering it. Rather, it arose spontaneously out of the sheer necessity for a money substance to facilitate economic exchange. Governments now control the issuance of money, but they did not invent it, and some form of money would continue to be used with or without government involvement. In this area as much as in any other, 'necessity' was truly the 'mother of invention.'"

3. Hutchinson (1992: 3) notes that in a modern economy we tend to take for granted the role that money plays as a *numeraire*—a measuring device in terms of which the market worth of all goods is evaluated and can be compared.

4. Similarly, Hutchinson (1992: 20) states that an efficient financial industry provides the medium of exchange without which specialization could hardly exist, and it provides a mechanism whereby any spending unit that does not choose to spend all of its current after-tax income on consumer goods (i.e., it chooses to save) may conveniently make that money available to other spending units who prefer to spend more than their current incomes. As he (1992: 20) concludes, "And, finally, in the process of accomplishing the latter, it makes available a procedure through which much of the nation's vital capital formation is financed."

5. These studies examine industrial countries. Barro's (1999) study includes both industrial and developing countries. Analysis of his expanded data set reveals that the relationship between central bank independence and inflation is weaker.

Chapter 3

Social Security and Private Saving: New Time Series Evidence

3.1. Introduction

In a recent study, Mitchell and Zeldes (1996) highlight the need for reform of the U.S. Social Security System. Near the time of this writing, its trustees have forecasted that contributions will fall below benefits in the year 2016, and that the system's trust fund will be exhausted by the year 2038. At that point, payroll taxes will be enough to pay only about 73-percent of benefits owed (Social Security Administration, 08/2001). The Mitchell-Zeldes article provides a framework for analyzing various plans to reform the system, including numerous privatization options. One of the catalysts behind many of the privatization plans being put forth by members of the U.S. House and U.S. Senate is the potential negative impact of the current Social Security system on national saving in the United States. In fact, the debate over the impact of the current system on national saving in America is one of the most well-known in the economics literature, dating back at least to Feldstein's (1974) seminal work. Feldstein points out that the "substitution factor"—which implies that the Social Security system and individual, private savings plans are viewed by American households as substitutes for one another (i.e., participation in the former lessens the incentive/desire to fund the latter)—plays a dominant role in shaping Americans' financial decisions regarding retirement.

Feldstein popularized the notion of "Social Security wealth" (hereafter SSW) in 1974. SSW represents, in simple form, the present value of retirement benefits that could be claimed by retirees and people in the American labor force. This seemingly complex present value (finance) concept is becoming increasingly clearer to American households with regard to Social Security benefits. In the past few years, the U.S. Social Security Administration began mailing *Social Security Statements* to individual Americans on an annual basis, usually three months prior to one's birthday. These statements contain many useful pieces of information, such as the fact that U.S. workers earn one credit for each $830 of wages or self-employed income, and once $3,320 has been earned, one's quota of four credits for the year has been met. Also, most individuals need 40 lifetime credits to become eligible for Social Security benefits in retirement, though younger individuals need fewer credits to qualify for disability and survivor benefits. Perhaps the most helpful information in the *Statements* is the provision of retirement income estimates, which are based on assumptions about a worker's lifetime earnings. According to a (hypothetical) recent *Statement* of this sort, a 32 year old worker in 2001 may be entitled to $13,944 in annual Social Security benefits upon retirement at age 67 (i.e., in the year 2036). That is, the individual's Social Security income in the year 2036 will be $13,944, other things constant (the present value of this amount, assuming an interest rate of 8-percent over time, is approximately $943). Then, there is the second year's (2037) retirement benefit to consider (i.e., its present value). How this person uses this information becomes a crucial element to the story. Will this person choose to supplement their Social Security plan with a private retirement account, or simply choose to rely solely on Social Security benefits? Based on a series of calculations such as this, our 32 year old might decide not to contribute any funds (or to contribute very little) to a private retirement account in the current year, 2001, and instead rely solely on payroll taxes paid into the Social Security System. Of course, the bigger the present value figure is for our individual, the more likely this may be his/her resulting decision. In this case, national saving in the U.S. is reduced from its potential, and the process of capital formation will be hindered.

These figures and computations are all, of course, subject to change based upon changes in earnings during one's working career, the chosen age of retirement, and the number retirement years enjoyed. Yet, these remain the types of calculations that U.S. workers make on an ongoing basis with regard to retirement planning. They are also important factors in an algorithm developed by Feldstein (which we detail below) for computing SSW for Americans. What remains is to examine the impact that figures such as these appearing in the annual *Statements* (and in Feldstein's algorithm) have on Americans' desire to substitute (supplement) Social Security support for (with) private retirement savings.

Using data from 1929-1971, Feldstein (1974) reports statistical evidence suggesting that the presence of Social Security wealth (SSW) in the U.S. contributed to at least a 40 percent decline in national savings (much of this would have been saved for retirement), and that when the lost savings due to the payroll tax contributions are included, national saving is reduced another nine percentage points. These figures, which are described in more detail later in this chapter, suggest—as in our hypothetical scenario above—that Americans view the Social Security program as a *substitute* for private retirement saving, and are thus using more (less) of their current disposable income for consumption (retirement saving) purposes.

In a later comment, Leimer and Lesnoy (1982) suggest that, (1) Feldstein's data set contained a computer error regarding the algorithm for computing SSW, (2) Feldstein's measure of SSW was conceptually flawed, and (3) Feldstein's results are sensitive to the particular time period used. After correcting for these problems, the Leimer-Lesnoy estimates (using 1930-1974 data) revealed an *insignificant* relationship between consumption (and thus saving) and Social Security wealth (SSW). However, in a reply Feldstein (1982) points out that by correcting the computer error, the presence of SSW alone (omitting the payroll tax effect) continues to reduce national saving in the U.S. by approximately 31-percent. When the data are expanded to cover the 1929-1976 period, the negative impact of SSW on national saving rises to 38-percent. If true, these latest estimates by Feldstein imply that capital formation and national income growth are significantly lower in the U.S. than they would be in the absence of the public pension system *or* possibly through privatization of that system. This is a view Feldstein (1995) continues to hold.

This chapter will not contest the possibility that there are, perhaps, superior ways to measure Social Security wealth (SSW), as Leimer and Lesnoy (1982) point out. This chapter will suggest the possibility that both the original Feldstein study in 1974, and the subsequent comment by Leimer-Lesnoy and reply by Feldstein (both in 1982) may all rely on spurious statistical estimates. The development of new macroeconomic statistical techniques to account for trends and random walks in time series data (Enders, 1995; Kennedy, 1998) occurred after the publication of these studies. Therefore, replication of the Feldstein results and re-testing with improved statistical techniques is a useful and timely endeavor, given the importance of the relationship between SSW and national saving. In the next section, we define some of the terms being used in this chapter (e.g., Social Security wealth, etc.) and provide a brief background of the elements of Feldstein's (1974) original model. This will be followed by a presentation of Feldstein's 1982 results and our own replications of his 1982 (and later) findings. After a review of the implications of the original models, we present new macroeconomic statistical techniques and regression estimates using data from the original time period. Lastly, we will present an analysis of the implications of our models that are based on modern statistical techniques.

3.2. Important Terms, Feldstein's Original Model, and Our Replications

The original model employed by Feldstein (1974) is a consumption function adapted from Ando and Modigliani (1963). This equation is presented as:

(3.1) $C = a_0 + b_1 SSW + b_2 W + b_3 YD + b_4 YD_{-1} + b_5 RE + \varepsilon$,

where C is real (i.e., inflation-adjusted) per-capita consumption (in the U.S. each year), YD is real per-capita disposable (after tax) income, YD_{-1} is the lag of real per-capita disposable income (i.e., previous year's real per-capita disposable income), W is the lag of real per-capita household wealth (i.e., household wealth accumulated through the end of the previous year) excluding social security wealth, RE is gross retained corporate earnings per capita, and SSW is gross Social Security wealth per-capita. SSW is used in *gross* form by Feldstein (1974 and 1982) because disposable income already excludes Social Security taxes (i.e., payroll taxes).

Feldstein's algorithm for computing SSW is somewhat more complex than depicted in our story above (see Feldstein, 1974), given that it includes assumptions regarding, (1) perceptions of the population concerning future increases in Social Security benefits over time, (2) the present value of future Social Security taxes to fund the system, (3) an individual's discount rate for future income, (4) the growth rate of real per-capita disposable income, (5) probabilities regarding survival to retirement age, and (6) special provisions for benefits differences for single women, working wives, and surviving spouses, among other facets not detailed here. These ideas are all affected, in some way, by current political trends (e.g., which political parties control Congress/The White House), advancements in medicines/nutrition (e.g., recent research just released posits that aspirin consumption lowers the risk of certain cancers among adults), and various changes in the economy. These relationships exist given that the variable SSW relates to passage of legislation in the political arena, life expectancy, and the dynamics of our macroeconomic environment.

All variables in equation (3.1) above are expected to be positively related to per-capita consumption. That is, disposable income (and its lag), business earnings (RE), and wealth (W) are all expected to positively influence purchase decisions by American consumers. For Feldstein's SSW, a positive finding would indicate that American consumers respond to increasing values of SSW by *consuming more*. Given the consumer's budget constraint—where disposable income equals consumption expenditures plus savings (i.e., $YD = C + S$)—any increase in C will be met with a decrease in S, or savings, holding YD constant. In this view, individuals will reduce all forms of private saving, including that for retirement, in the face of higher current consumption expenditures that result from the presence of the Social Security system. On the other hand, a negative finding for SSW would yield the opposite interpretation—that is, lower levels of private consumption would result from increasing values of SSW, thus indicating a "complementary" relationship between public and private retirement programs. Individuals might respond to the existence of one (i.e., Social Security) by increasing their funding of the other (i.e., private, individual retirement accounts), perhaps in an effort to retire at a younger age or retire with a more comfortable lifestyle. The empirical models will establish the dominant relationship among these competing possibilities.

Feldstein's original statistical model employed data from 1929-1971 (exclusive of 1941-1946 for World War II). Some summary statistics from his original study are presented in Table 3.1, and his regression results are presented as version (1) in Table 3.2. The autonomous

Table 3.1
Social Security Wealth
(Billions of Constant 1971 Dollars)

| | Gross Wealth | | Net Wealth | | |
| | SSWG1 | SSWG5 | SSWN1 | SSWN5 | GNP |
Year	(1)	(2)	(3)	(4)	(5)
1940	235	70	145	25	321
1950	442	153	227	36	503
1955	690	270	366	81	620
1960	917	380	493	122	691
1965	1,397	596	805	234	875
1971	2,029	875	1,162	342	1,050

Notes: Feldstein converted the SSW values to constant dollars by the implicit price deflator for personal consumption expenditures. The choice of "discount factor" is indicated by a final number in the name of the variable (e.g., SSWG1 refers to the gross social security variable using a net discount factor of 1.01 (see Feldstein, 1974: 916).

Source: Feldstein (1974: 915).

Table 3.2
Regression Estimates of Consumption Functions with Social Security Wealth: Equation 3.1

Version	Period	Source	SSW Variable	SSW	W	YD	YD$_{-1}$	RE
(1)	1929-1971	Feldstein	Old	0.021	0.014	0.530	0.120	0.356
				(0.006)	(0.004)	(0.047)	(0.035)	(0.074)
(2)	1929-1971	Feldstein	Corrected	0.015	0.011	0.648	0.109	0.118
				(0.010)	(0.005)	(0.058)	(0.045)	(0.089)
(3)	1937-1971	Replication	Corrected	0.023	-0.019	0.647[a]	0.063	0.658[c]

				(0.028)	(0.013)	(0.111)	(0.068)	(0.353)
(4)	1929-1974	Feldstein	Corrected	0.011	0.009	0.686	0.100	0.066
				(0.010)	(0.006)	(0.057)	(0.044)	(0.078)
(5)	1937-1974	Replication	Corrected	0.052[b]	0.020[c]	0.623[a]	0.012	-0.276
				(0.023)	(0.014)	(0.157)	(0.093)	(0.405)
(6)	1929-1974	Feldstein	Revised	0.017	0.011	0.645	0.103	0.132
				(0.008)	(0.005)	(0.057)	(0.041)	(0.072)
(7)	1937-1974	Replication	Revised	0.031[b]	0.022[c]	0.633[a]	0.030	-0.134
				(0.013)	(0.014)	(0.149)	(0.091)	(0.409)
(8)	1929-1976	Feldstein	Corrected	0.002	0.007	0.743	0.094	0.024
				(0.011)	(0.006)	(0.062)	(0.052)	(0.088)
(9)	1937-1976	Replication	Corrected	0.049[b]	0.019[c]	0.629[a]	0.011	-0.268
				(0.022)	(0.014)	(0.144)	(0.087)	(0.375)
(10)	1929-1976	Feldstein	Revised	0.018	0.009	0.671	0.090	0.067
				(0.009)	(0.006)	(0.065)	(0.048)	(0.077)
(11)	1937-1976	Replication	Revised	0.024[b]	0.020[c]	0.675[a]	0.025	-0.186
				(0.012)	(0.014)	(0.138)	(0.087)	(0.384)

Note: The dependent variable is, again, C. The numbers in parentheses below the parameter estimates are standard errors. The superscripts attached to the parameter estimates (for our replications only)—a, b and c—denote significance at the 0.01, 0.05 and 0.10 level, respectively, for a one-tailed test (See Leamer, 1978; Kennedy, 1998).

Sources: Feldstein (1974 and 1982) and the authors.

consumption estimates for these models, along with Durbin-Watson *d*-statistics, are presented in Table 3.3.

Table 3.3
Autonomous Consumption and Durbin-Watson d-Statistics: Equation 3.1

Version	Autonomous Consumption Estimates	Durbin-Watson d
(1)	228 [31]	1.82
(2)	236 [55]	1.23
(3)	369[a] [109]	1.99
(4)	198 [55]	1.40
(5)	286[b] [126]	1.93
(6)	247 [50]	1.31
(7)	238[b] [104]	2.04
(8)	139 [60]	1.37
(9)	295[b] [119]	2.36
(10)	240 [58]	1.29
(11)	222[b] [101]	2.43

Notes: The numbers in brackets next to the parameter estimates are standard errors. The superscripts attached to the parameter estimates (for our replications only)—a and b—denote significance at the 0.01, 0.05 level, respectively, for a one-tailed test (See Leamer, 1978; Kennedy, 1998).
Sources: Feldstein (1974 and 1982) and the authors.

All of the variables within Feldstein's (1974) original Ordinary Least Squares (OLS) regression model (see version 1 of Table 3.2) retain the expected positive signs. Additionally, the parameter estimate for SSW is significantly greater than zero, and quite large in magnitude (0.021). However, as Leimer and Lesnoy (1982) pointed out, Feldstein's computation of the SSW variable originally contained a computer error. Corrected results over the same time period were later published by Feldstein (1982).

These "corrected" OLS estimates are presented as version (2) of Table 3.2. Here, the SSW estimate falls to 0.015, and is only *marginally* significant.

Our work re-estimates (replicates) the "corrected" Feldstein model using data from 1937-1971.[1] Our OLS results are presented as version (3) of Table 3.2. These results are somewhat similar to those of Feldstein, although the size of the RE parameter is much larger than in Feldstein's estimation, *and* it is significantly different from zero in our model. The marginal propensity to consume, given by the parameter estimate for YD, is similar across our two models, however the variables W and YD_{-1} are *in*significant in our replication. Finally, the coefficient attaching to SSW in our first replication, though larger in magnitude (0.023) than Feldstein's estimate, is *in*significant as well. All of the results so far regarding SSW, though, do support the notion that the U.S. Social Security system works as a pension *substitute*, discouraging private, individual saving for retirement purposes (given the positive sign attaching to SSW in the models). As Chapter 2 indicates, given the positive relationship between national saving and private economic investment, this reduction in private saving hinders capital formation and economic growth.

Table 3.2 also presents several other "corrected" versions of equation (3.1) estimated by Feldstein (1982) that are also re-estimated (replicated) in the current study. These include extending the data set sequentially to 1974, and then to 1976. Feldstein's results for these extensions are presented as versions (4) and (8) of Table 3.2. In both cases, the OLS estimate for SSW is positive, though quite smaller (0.011 and 0.002, respectively) than the 0.021 estimate of the original Feldstein (1974) study; both are also statistically *in*significant. Our own replications accounting for these time-series extensions are presented in Table 3.2 as versions (5) and (9). The parameter estimates for SSW in these replications of Feldstein's extensions are quite large (0.052 and 0.049, respectively) and statistically *significant*. In fact, they are much larger than Feldstein's original "uncorrected" (old) estimate of 0.021.

Lastly, in his reply to Leimer and Lesnoy, Feldstein (1982) noted that in 1972 the U.S. Congress enacted a major change in the method for calculating and adjusting Social Security benefits. This change included an increase in annual retirement benefits based on a percentage rise in the Consumer Price Index (CPI) as well as a permanent increase of 20-percent in annual benefits.[2] In an attempt to adjust the algorithm for SSW to account for these changes, Feldstein suggests,

> "…[increasing] all social security benefits by 20 percent for the years beginning with 1972 and thus…calculate an aggregate SSW variable for all such years that is greater than it would be if the old algorithm were used instead. This 20 percent rise would reflect congressional intent and would ignore the unpredictable problems of double indexing…a 20 percent rise would also correspond to the actual rise in the ratio of social security benefits to average income between the pre-1972 years and the later period." (Feldstein, 1982: 635)

Some of the data resulting from this "revision" by Feldstein (1982: 641) are presented in Table 3.4 below.

Table 3.4
Revised Social Security Wealth
(Revised Series in Billions of 1972 Dollars)

Year	Revised SSW Series
1937	160.400
1939	236.300
1948	464.100
1950	489.700
1952	629.500
1955	758.000
1958	880.900

1960	946.400
1962	1,052.000
1965	1,287.700
1968	1,545.900
1970	1,679.200
1974	2,404.560
1975	2,318.760

Source: Feldstein (1982: 641).

This revision necessitated two additional OLS regression models, which were presented by Feldstein (1982) and are also included in Table 3.2 as "revised" versions (6) and (10). In both, the coefficient attaching to SSW is approximately the size (0.017 and 0.018, respectively) of the "corrected" coefficient estimated using the 1929-1971 data (0.015). Both of these coefficients are statistically significant, however. Versions (7) and (11) of Table 3.2 contain our own modified replications of the "revised" Feldstein model. Here, the estimates for SSW are also positive (0.031 and 0.024, respectively), significant, and quite large—similar in size to (or even larger than) Feldstein's original estimate of 0.021.

Next, as the information in Table 3.3 points out, the OLS estimates for autonomous consumption (in the original Feldstein studies) range from a low of 139 to a high of 247; all are statistically significant (although they are not necessarily denoted as such in Table 3.3). Among our modified replications, estimates for autonomous consumption range from a low of 222 to a high of 369; there is, therefore, some overlap in Feldstein's autonomous consumption estimates and those from our own modified replications. Again, the estimates for autonomous consumption in our modified replications are all significant at the 0.05 level, or better.

Durbin-Watson statistics are also reported in Table 3.3 for Feldstein's original work and our own modified replications. As the table makes clear, our replications are relatively free from serial correlation problems; in at least some of the Feldstein versions, serial correlation is likely to pose a statistical problem. Lastly, in all of the models presented in Table 3.2, adjusted R-square measures are greater than or equal to 0.98.

As Leimer and Lesnoy (1982) pointed out, Feldstein's results are perhaps somewhat sensitive to the particular time period under consideration. However, we found no evidence of a *negative* relationship between SSW and C as do some of the Leimer-Lesnoy regression equations, and most of our modified replications produce *statistically significant* and somewhat *larger* coefficients for SSW using an alternative time period to that of the original Feldstein models. Next, we examine some empirical predictions on Social Security's impact on national saving using the Feldstein models and our own modified replications.

3.3. Examining Social Security's Impact on National Saving

As Feldstein suggests in his 1982 study, the marginal propensity to consume disposable income is 0.671 (see version 1 of Table 3.2), the marginal propensity to save is 0.329, and the marginal propensity to spend/consume SSW is 0.018, as given by the parameter estimates in the regressions. Given that SSW amounted to $3,208 billion (in current dollars) for 1976, the data suggest that the existence of the Social Security system—viewed as a "substitute" by Americans—reduced national saving by $58 billion, or by 38 percent of is potential size (i.e., $153 billion), based on the fact that total private saving in the U.S. during 1976 was $95 billion.[3] This reduction also amounts to about 3.4-percent of GNP in 1976 (which was $1,702 billion). When the loss in savings due to payroll taxes to fund the system, which amounted to $63 billion in 1976, are included, a further reduction in savings of $21 billion is produced.[4] This raises the reduction in potential savings to 45 percent.

Using the same macroeconomic data for 1976, our modified replication using "revised" estimates for SSW and data from 1937-1976 (see version 11 of Table 3.2) suggests that the direct reduction in national saving, from a marginal propensity to consume/spend SSW of 0.024, was approximately $77 billion. This amounts to a reduction in total private saving (from its potential) in 1976 of about 45-percent, and the level of reduced savings represents about 4.5-percent of GNP for 1976. When payroll taxes are included, total savings are reduced a further $20 billion in 1976. These results point out that the presence of the Social Security system wealth (SSW) reduced national saving (from its potential) by about 50-percent; all of the results described above are summarized in Table 3.5.

Table 3.5

Summary of Social Security's Estimated Impact on National Saving

Period	Table 3.2 Version	$-Reduction in National Saving	%-Reduction in National Saving
1929-1976	Version (10)	$58 billion (w/out pr. taxes)	38% (w/out pr. taxes)
1937-1976	Version (11)	$77 billion (w/out pr. taxes)	45% (w/out pr. taxes)
1929-1976	Version (10)	$79 Billion (w/ pr. taxes)	45% (w/ pr. taxes)
1937-1976	Version (11)	$97 Billion (w/ pr. taxes)	50% (w/ pr. taxes)

Sources: Feldstein (1982) and the authors.

The numbers here are substantial, but may simply represent unreliable or spurious regression results due to trends in models that employ macroeconomic variables and time series data. These problems are suggested in a series of works that has appeared, for the most part, in the economics literature since the Feldstein/Leimer-Lesnoy debates concerning Social Security. They are detailed in the next section, and further empirical verification of Feldstein's hypothesis is attempted.

3.4. Reconciling the Debate with New Statistical Procedures

Most time series, particularly those employing macroeconomic variables, contain data that are non-stationary (Nelson and Plosser, 1982). The use of non-stationary data may produce spurious or unreliable regression results. Therefore, to avoid such problems it is necessary that the variables in equation (3.1) above are tested for stationarity. Following Nelson and Plosser (1982), an Augmented Dickey-Fuller test was conducted to ensure stationarity (see also Elder and Kennedy, 2001; Mixon, Sawyer, and Upadhyaya, 2002). This involves estimating the following regression, and carrying out unit root tests:

$$(3.2) \Delta X_t = a + bt + cX_{t-1} + \sum_{i=1}^{n} d_i \Delta X_{t-i} + e_t.$$

Here, X is the variable under consideration, Δ is the first difference operator, t is a time trend, and e is a stationary error term. If the null hypothesis, that $c=0$, is not rejected, the variable series contains a unit root and is non-stationary (in which case the results discussed above are likely spurious). The optimal lag length in equation (3.2) above is identified by verifying the presence of a white noise error term. In addition to the Augmented Dickey-Fuller test, a Phillips-Perron test (Phillips, 1987; Phillips and Perron, 1988) is conducted (see Mixon, Sawyer and Upadhyaya, 2002). All of these tests are used to examine the three different time-series employed in our modified replications of Feldstein's work. The Phillips-Perron tests indicate that some of the variable series are stationary in level form, although the Augmented Dickey-Fuller tests fail to confirm some of these findings. The findings for the 1937-1976 period, the 1937-1974 period, and the 1937-1971 period are reported in Table 3.6, Table 3.7, and Table 3.8, respectively.

Table 3.6
Unit Root Tests
Time Series: 1937-1976

Variable	Augmented Dickey-Fuller		Phillips-Perron	
	Level	FD	Level	FD
C	-2.87	-4.98***	-3.91**	-8.23***
YD	-2.82	-5.83***	-4.11**	-8.58***
W	-3.19	-4.61***	-3.88**	-7.12***
RE	-3.03	-5.31***	-3.13	-5.73***
SSW corrected	-2.06	-4.75***	-1.79	-4.99***
SSW revised	-1.14	-4.50***	-1.47	-4.93***

Notes: ***(**) denotes the 0.01(0.05) level of significance; FD=first difference form.

Table 3.7
Unit Root Tests
Time Series: 1937-1974

Variable	Augmented Dickey-Fuller		Phillips-Perron	
	Level	FD	Level	FD
C	-1.83	-4.66***	-2.96	-7.20***
YD	-2.79	-5.74***	-3.94**	-8.03***
W	-3.10	-4.08**	-3.46*	-5.75***
RE	-2.78	-4.67***	-2.58	-4.55***
SSW corrected	-1.42	-4.52***	-1.06	-4.98***
SSW revised	-1.12	-4.45***	-0.77	-4.93***

Notes: ***(**)[*] denotes the 0.01(0.05)[0.10] level of significance; FD=first difference form.

Table 3.8
Unit Root Tests
Time Series: 1937-1971

Variable	Augmented Dickey-Fuller		Phillips-Perron	
	Level	FD	Level	FD
C	-2.84	-4.89***	-3.89**	-7.77***
YD	-2.78	-4.39***	-3.70**	-6.21***
W	-2.77	-3.24*	-3.37*	-6.81***
RE	-3.05	-4.18**	-2.51	-4.84***
SSW corrected	-2.82	-3.69**	-2.35	-6.08***

Notes: ***(**)[*] denotes the 0.01(0.05)[0.10] level of significance; FD=first difference form.

New research indicates that the power of these unit root tests is somewhat low. Also, because these tests often indicate that a series contains a unit root, they were conducted on the first-differences (i.e., "changes in") of the same data series (Enders, 1995: 251-254). All of the data series were ultimately found to be stationary in first-difference form.

After establishing the stationarity of the data series (in first-difference form), we conducted cointegration tests (Johansen, 1988; Johansen and Juselius, 1990) to explore any long run equilibrium relationship among the variables.[5] Johansen's cointegration test results for the 1937-1976 period are reported in Table 3.9. As reported, the null hypothesis of "no cointegration" is

Table 3.9
Johansen's Cointegration Test
Time Series: 1937-1976

H_0:	Likelihood Ratio [corrected SSW]	Likelihood Ratio [revised SSW]	5% critical value	1% critical value
$\gamma=0$	154.05**	162.72**	94.15	103.18
$\gamma\leq1$	102.77**	105.87**	68.52	76.07
$\gamma\leq2$	56.69**	59.09**	47.21	54.46
$\gamma\leq3$	30.61*	30.97*	29.68	35.65
$\gamma\leq4$	13.25	10.81	15.41	20.04
$\gamma\leq5$	0.45	0.05	3.76	6.65

Note: **(*) denotes rejection of the null hypothesis at the 0.01(0.05) level.

rejected in our estimations. Tests for the other time periods under consideration in this study (i.e., 1937-1974, and 1937-1971) are reported in Tables 3.10 and 3.11. The results presented for

Table 3.10
Johansen's Cointegration Test
Time Series: 1937-1974

H_0:	Likelihood Ratio [corrected SSW]	Likelihood Ratio [revised SSW]	5% critical value	1% critical value
$\gamma=0$	145.96**	157.80**	94.15	103.18
$\gamma\leq1$	90.71**	96.61**	68.52	76.07
$\gamma\leq2$	47.07	50.96*	47.21	54.46
$\gamma\leq3$	23.45	23.25	29.68	35.65
$\gamma\leq4$	9.63	8.56	15.41	20.04
$\gamma\leq5$	2.10	1.19	3.76	6.65

Note: **(*) denotes rejection of the null hypothesis at the 0.01(0.05) level.

Table 3.11
Johansen's Cointegration Test
Time Series: 1937-1971

H_0:	Likelihood Ratio [corrected SSW]	5% critical value	1% critical value
$\gamma=0$	139.67**	94.15	103.18
$\gamma \leq 1$	93.64**	68.52	76.07
$\gamma \leq 2$	52.31*	47.21	54.46
$\gamma \leq 3$	25.96	29.68	35.65
$\gamma \leq 4$	8.40	15.41	20.04
$\gamma \leq 5$	0.08	3.76	6.65

Note: **(*) denotes rejection of the null hypothesis at the 0.01(0.05) level.

the two alternative time periods confirm those for 1937-1976. Therefore, following Engle and Granger (1987), an error-correction model is used to estimate the Feldstein consumption equation containing our variable of interest, SSW.. This involves use of equation (3.1) above in first-difference form, and with the addition of an error-correction representation (EC) to the original set of regressors. The error-correction model of equation (3.1) to be estimated is given:

(3.3) $\Delta C = a_0 + a_1 \Delta SSW + a_2 \Delta W + a_3 \Delta YD + a_4 \Delta YD_{-1} + a_5 \Delta RE + a_6 EC + v$.

The error correction term (EC) in equation (3.3) is the lag of the estimated error of equation (3.1) above, and in all estimations it is expected to carry a negative and significant sign. The results of the error-correction models for various sample periods and definitions of SSW are reported in Table 3.12. The Durbin-Watson *d*-statistics, and adjusted R-square measures for these models

Table 3.12
Error-Correction Models of Consumption Functions with Social Security Wealth

Version	Period	SSW Variable	ΔSSW	ΔW	ΔYD	ΔYD_{-1}	ΔRE	EC
(1)	1937-1971	Corrected	0.05	-0.02[b]	0.53[a]	0.03	1.22[a]	-1.13[a]
			(0.043)	(0.008)	(0.086)	(0.067)	(0.320)	(0.231)
(2)	1937-1974	Corrected	0.02	0.03[a]	0.58[a]	0.01	0.34	-1.12[a]
			(0.047)	(0.012)	(0.118)	(0.125)	(0.405)	(0.218)
(3)	1937-1974	Revised	0.01	0.03[a]	0.58[a]	0.02	0.48	-1.15[a]
			(0.016)	(0.011)	(0.111)	(0.071)	(0.400)	(0.222)
(4)	1937-1976	Corrected	0.04[c]	0.03[a]	0.59[a]	0.02	0.03	-1.21[a]
			(0.029)	(0.009)	(0.114)	(0.087)	(0.043)	(0.192)
(5)	1937-1976	Revised	0.03[c]	0.04[a]	0.64[a]	0.03	0.05	-1.26[a]
			(0.021)	(0.013)	(0.111)	(0.073)	(0.357)	(0.195)

Notes: The dependent variable is, again, C. The numbers in parentheses below the parameter estimates are standard errors. The superscripts attached to the parameter estimates—a, b and c—denote significance at the 0.01, 0.05, and 0.10 levels for a one-tailed test. Each model above produces an adjusted R^2 of at least 0.77.

are presented in Table 3.13.

Table 3.13
Durbin-Watson d-Statistics and Adjusted R-squares: Equation 3.3

Version	Durbin-Watson d	Adjusted R^2
(1)	1.72	0.89
(2)	1.94	0.77
(3)	1.96	0.77
(4)	2.21	0.78
(5)	2.18	0.77

Note: The versions denoted above refer to those in Table 3.10.

Version (1) of Table 3.12 presents a modified replication of the "corrected" Feldstein model, using the error-correction procedure and data from 1937-1971. Several anomalous results are shown there, such as the *sign* and *significance* of ΔW, the *magnitude* of the significant coefficient attaching to ΔRE, the *magnitude* of the ΔYD coefficient and the *insignificance* of the variable ΔSSW. Versions (4) and (5), however, which use the 1937-1976 time series, produce results similar to those of Feldstein and the replications presented earlier in this chapter.[6] In version (5), the coefficient attaching to ΔYD is 0.64, while that for ΔW is positive (0.03) and significant. ΔRE retains a coefficient of 0.05, although it is *insignificant*. The coefficient attaching to ΔSSW in version (5) is 0.03, and it is significant at the 0.10 level. It version (4), this estimate climbs to 0.04 (and is again significant).

As Table 3.13 points out, each of the models has a high degree of explanatory power. Adjusted R-square statistics range from a low of 0.77, in versions (2), (3), and (5), to a high of 0.89 (version 1). Also, the Durbin-Watson scores fail to indicate the presence of serial correlation problems in our replications. This is especially true for version (5) of Table 3.12, which we make use of in further analysis presented in the next section.

3.5. Re-examining Social Security's Impact on National Saving

The results presented for the "revised" SSW from 1937-1976 (version 5 of Table 3.12) suggest that (1) a $1 billion change in real disposable income results in a change in real consumption of $640 million, (2) a $1 billion change in real household wealth results in a change in real consumption of $40 million, (3) a $1 billion change in real corporate retained earnings results in a change in real consumption of $50 million, and (4) a $1 billion change in real SSW results in a change in real consumption of $30 million. The model also suggests that an increase in payroll tax receipts of $1 billion results in a change in real consumption -$640 million and a change in real national saving of -$360 million. Using version (5) of Table 3.12 and the current dollars numbers for 1976 provided by Feldstein (1982), the presence of Social Security wealth ($3,208 billion in 1976) reduced national saving by $96 billion in 1976 (5.6-percent of 1976 GNP), or by 50-percent of its potential, given that total private saving in 1976 was $95 billion. The payroll tax revenue (for 1976) of $63 billion reduced national saving (from its potential) by an additional $23 billion, for a total cut of $119 billion. This represents 56-percent of the *potential* total private saving in the U.S. for 1976. These numbers are very similar to those that were produced from the simple OLS (modified) replications of the Feldstein consumption model detailed earlier in this chapter, and are also remarkably consistent with Feldstein's most recent finding of a near 60-percent reduction using data from 1930-1992 (Feldstein, 1996). They are presented, along with those from equation (4) of Table 3.12, below in Table 3.14.

Table 3.14
Summary of Social Security's *Re-estimated* Impact on National Saving

Period	Table 3.12 Version	$-Reduction in National Saving	%-Reduction in National Saving
1937-1976	Version (4)	$128 billion (w/out pr. taxes)	57% (w/out pr. taxes)
1937-1976	Version (5)	$96 billion (w/out pr. taxes)	50% (w/out pr. taxes)
1937-1976	Version (4)	$154 billion (w/ pr. taxes)	62% (w/ pr. taxes)
1937-1976	Version (5)	$119 billion (w/ pr. taxes)	56% (w/ pr. taxes)

Sources: The authors.

The inclusion of stationarity and cointegration tests highlights the sensitivity of the estimates to the time period and the definition employed for SSW ("corrected" or "revised"), as in Leimer and Lesnoy (1982). The two versions of the error-correction model that cover the entire time period (1937-1976) produce estimates that are compatible with those produced using OLS by Feldstein (1982 and 1996). In these models, the negative impact of the Social Security system on national saving in the U.S. appears to real *and* quite large in magnitude, as Martin Feldstein originally pointed out over 25 years ago. This reduction implies that both private investment expenditures and economic growth have been stunted in the U.S., *ceteris paribus*, since the 1930's when SSW first appeared.

3.6. Final Thoughts

This chapter has updated an important debate in the economics literature regarding the impact of the current Social Security system on national saving in the United States. When the macroeconomic data used by Feldstein (1974; 1982)—in a now famous series of works that estimates a consumption function with Social Security wealth—are subjected to various tests for stationarity, the conclusions drawn by Feldstein over 25 years ago are reconfirmed. The statistical techniques used in this chapter were not as widely available during that time, although the techniques would have shed light on the fact that the data used by Feldstein and others were non-stationary. Some re-estimations presented here using these procedures suggest that the existence of the Social Security system wealth reduces national saving from 38- to 62-percent, depending on the definition of Social Security wealth that is employed and on whether payroll tax receipts are included. In either case, these costs are substantial. We turn next to additional, and often hidden, costs associated with the U.S. Social Security system. These revolve around lobbying effort to secure access—by individuals and interest groups—to the federal dollars that reside in the system's Trust Fund. Before detailing these costs, we review some of the basic elements of rent seeking and public choice theory in the next chapter.

Notes to Chapter 3

1.   The fact that our data series (1937-1971&76) differs from that of Feldstein (1929-1971&76), although our vector of exogenous variables is the same as Feldstein's, makes our study a modified replication. The time period 1937-1971&76 was chosen to avoid any possible spurious regression results associated with using observations where SSW was estimated as $0.00 (i.e., from 1929-1937, before the existence of Social Security Wealth or implementation of the program). By using only the years where SSW is non-zero (i.e., 1937-1971&76, exclusive of the WWII years), we attempted to avoid use of regression estimates based on such a large discrete jump in the SSW measure. In doing so, our work

also (partly) addresses the time frame concerns expressed by Leimer and Lesnoy (1982).

2. These are the types of legislative actions individuals take into account in assessing the viability of viewing the Social Security system as a "substitute" (or "complement") to private, individual saving for retirement years. As history often suggests, such legislative actions can work in the other direction (i.e., 20 percent reductions are also possible). For instance, a 1983 change in the Social Security law raised the full retirement age (gradually) from 65 to 67 for people born in 1960 or later. For those born before 1938, the full retirement age is 65 (Social Security Administration, 08/2001).

3. These figures are found by multiplying the relevant regression coefficients by the U.S. data for the particular year in question (here, 1976). The notion here is that American consumers are spending disposable income they would instead be saving for retirement in the absence of a federally mandated retirement program (i.e., Social Security).

4. The notion here is that American consumers would be spending 0.671, and saving 0.329, of this $63 billion in payroll taxes they are relinquishing to the Social Security system.

5. Although not common in public choice studies, these types of tests are indeed useful when dealing with macroeconomic variables/time series data. See Mixon, Gibson and Upadhyaya (2000) for an example of their use in public choice.

6. It should be noted that the error-correction loses one observation. A small sample likely plagues all of the models presented in this chapter. Due to the small sample size, we chose to employ a significance test based on a 0.10 level of significance (see Kennedy, 1998; Leamer, 1978).

Chapter 4

The Rent Seeking Model in Public Choice: A Brief Review

4.1. Introduction and Background

What do tariffs, monopolies and theft have in common? As Gordon Tullock's (1967) work suggests, they each involve resource costs—or social opportunity costs—resulting from attempts by individuals/groups to redistribute income (or goods, resources, etc.) from one party to another. In the tariff case (i.e., a tax on imported goods), income is redistributed from consumers of international commodities in country A to the producers of those commodities (domestically) in country A. In the monopoly case, a similar story gets told—that is, income is redistributed from consumers of the monopolized good to its producers. Lastly, with theft income goes from the victim to the perpetrator.

Perhaps the first two cases above are most interesting, given that the redistributions are sanctioned by government. Textile (or steel, etc.) producers lobby federal legislators in Washington for protection, often in the form of import tariffs against foreign competition/products. If successful, the resulting higher prices in the domestic market bring greater profits and producer surplus to domestic textile (or steel, etc.) producers. In the latter case, most local monopolies that we face on a daily basis, such as the local electric utility or cable television company, are the result of public franchises (or licensing restrictions), wherein governments protect these entities from competition within (generally) a geographic area. Again, the result is higher "domestic" (i.e., in the relevant geographic area) prices of the product and a transfer of wealth from consumers (consumer surplus) to producers (producer surplus/profit).[1]

With these insights, public choice scholars have supplemented, during the second half of the 20th century, the traditional notion of so-called deadweight losses due to monopoly (or even tariff protections) with the now well-known theory of rent seeking.[2] Tullock (1967), Krueger (1974), and Posner (1975) all expanded the traditional notion of deadweight loss to include competing resource investments to obtain monopoly rents/profits.[3] This series of works suggests the following propositions: businesses will devote real resources (usually thought to be campaign contributions and other forms of *overt* political support) to lobbying within the political process to obtain governmentally-granted monopoly rights/privileges, and this resource investment is (normatively) considered socially unproductive.[4] Any rents to be derived from the transfer from consumers to producers will be dissipated as firms and individuals compete for the monopoly rights (Mixon and Ladner, 1998: 30). These propositions are supported with an illustration and further empirical evidence below.

4.2. The Social Costs of Rent Seeking: An Illustration and Empirical Evidence

It is usually instructive to support these concepts with an illustration. Consider the case of a cable television monopoly. Assume that a licensing or franchising authority, such as the city council, chooses to create a localized or geographic monopoly in the provision of cable television. Assume further that net revenue to the holder of the cable monopoly is $2 million per year, and that the license has a 2-year lifetime (subject to renewal). In this simple case, one may compute the present value of the two-year profit stream to the potential monopolist. Here, assuming a 6-percent rate of interest, the figures are $1,886,800 (PV of year 1 profit) and $1,780,000 (PV of year 2 profit), and they sum to $3,666,800. Assume now that 5 potential licensees are vying for the CATV monopoly, each with a one-in-five (four-in-five) chance of winning (not winning) the prize (i.e., the license, and thus, the $3,666,800). In this case, over a large number of simulated outcomes, each would win one-fifth of the time (and get $3,666,800) and each would lose four-fifths of the time (and get $0). Therefore, average or expected earnings in this case for each participant will be one-fifth of the license's value, or $733,360. This figure becomes each applicant's rent seeking investment rule; that is, each will have an incentive to devote real resources (time, income, etc.)—up to his/her expected earnings (i.e., $733,360)—in order to secure this monopoly position or privilege. In sum, $3,666,800, or the entire monopoly profit area, will be dissipated by the five potential licensees (the figures used in the above analysis are presented in Table 4.1).[5] This aggregate investment represents the (normative) case regarding the social opportunity costs of rent seeking in the public choice paradigm, given that the resources invested in securing the monopoly privilege could have been put to more socially productive uses.

Table 4.1
Rent Seeking and Rent Dissipation: A Hypothetical CATV Monopoly

Monopoly Type: Local CATV provision
Expected Monopoly Rents: $2,000,000/yr.
License Length/Life: 2 years (renewable)
Interest Rate over 2 year period: 6%
Present Value of Expected Monopoly Rents: $3,666,800
Number of Applicants for CATV License: 5
Odds of Winning License Contract: 1/5
Expected Earnings (from selection process): $733,360/applicant
Rent Seeking Expenditure Rule: $733,360/applicant
Total Rent Seeking Expenditures: $3,666,800 (i.e., $733,360 × 5)
PV of Expected Monopoly Rents minus Total Rent Seeking Expenditures: $0

Source: the Authors.

Tullock (1989) points out that public choice scholars have also used government transfers (i.e., government expenditures) more or less interchangeably with monopolistic restrictions in building the rent seeking argument. To a large extent, both are the result of rent-seeking activity and normally involve large inefficiencies. Converting the formal analysis of rent seeking to deal with government spending/transfers instead of monopoly restrictions is fairly straightforward and has been accomplished (see Tullock, 1970, 1971, 1989).[6] In a further extension, constitutional economists have also argued that rent seeking (at the fiscal stage) is an inevitable phenomenon in majoritarian democracy (see Sutter, 1995), and general reform of the political system to mitigate the social costs of rent seeking is possible (if at all) only at the constitutional level (Sutter, 1998).[7] What do the data with regard to rent seeking effort reveal? Some prominent writers have wondered at the low levels *observed* rent seeking (empirically) as a percentage of the total politically-directed transfers in the U.S.

and have questioned the theory that rents are fully dissipated (for details see Laband, 1991; Laband and Sophocleus, 1991; 1992; Tullock, 1997; 1998). Tullock (1980) himself has questioned whether rents are fully dissipated due to rent seeking costs and, more recently, maintains that "the rent seeking industry is surprisingly small (1989: 3)." Tullock notes that "…by visiting Washington and thinking about the size of injury inflicted upon our economy by activities there, anyone should be convinced that there is a real problem. Why should investment in influencing government action appear to have such high payoffs? (1989: 4)"[8]

There is a wealth of empirical evidence in the economics literature (e.g., Stratmann, 1991; 1995; Grier and Munger, 1991; Snyder, 1990; 1993; Mixon and Wilkinson, 1999; Lott, 2000) that is consistent with the view that campaign contributions are *overt* methods of providing favors to legislators, who in turn support rent seeking activities (Mixon and Ladner, 1998: 30). Several studies have attempted to bridge the gap noted above by Tullock with empirical estimates of *unobserved* in-kind rent seeking efforts in society (Mixon, Laband, and Ekelund, 1994; Sollars, 1996; Dascher, 2000; Sobel and Garrett, 2002; Gibson, 2003).[9] These studies have found significant rent seeking investments in the form *personal services* provided to legislators and government officials by individuals and interest groups. Many of these items are listed below (with supporting empirical studies) in Table 4.2,, along with items based on conceptual arguments in Laband and McClintock (2001).[10]

Table 4.2
Forms of In-Kind Rent Seeking Effort

Form	Supporting Study(ies)
Business patronage	Laband and McClintock (2001)
Discounted real estate sale	Laband and McClintock (2001)
Escort services	Sobel and Garrett (2002)

Golf excursions	Mixon, Laband, and Ekelund (1994); Mixon and McKenzie (1996)
Limousine services	Mixon (1995)
Massage services	Sobel and Garrett (2002)
Miscellaneous services	Sollars (1996); Dascher (2000) Sobel and Garrett (2002)
Post-elective employment	Gibson (2003)
Restaurant (fancy) dining	Mixon, Laband, and Ekelund (1994); Mixon and McKenzie (1996); Sobel and Garrett (2002)
Speaking invitations (with fees)	Laband and McClintock (2001)
Sports/Recreation club memberships	Sobel and Garrett (2002)
Sports arena suites	Laband and McClintock (2001)
Third party charitable donations	Laband and McClintock (2001)
Tuition scholarship/college acceptances	Laband and McClintock (2001)

All of the services listed by the work detailed in Table 4.2 supplement the traditional, more *overt* methods of rent seeking; the volume of empirical work presented in Table 4.2 is also supportive of the pioneering research of Tullock (1959) and Buchanan and Tullock (1962) on the social costs of rent seeking. These findings on in-kind rent seeking effort are also consistent with Lipford's (2001) discussion of the hidden costs of off-budget government spending and a general lack of transparency in U.S. fiscal policy.[11]

All things considered, the social costs of rent seeking are likely to be enormous.[12] We might never know its full extent given that a substantial portion of its costs emanate from *unobservable* or *unmeasurable* (at least accurately) in-kind political favors and perquisites.

4.2. Concluding Comments

This chapter has provided a brief look at the rent seeking element of the public choice tradition. This concept points out that real resources are devoted to lobbying government and other entities that have the institutional authority to transfer wealth within society. As Gordon Tullock and other public choice pioneers have suggested, this lobbying effort—and the resources that it wastefully consumes—represents a social opportunity cost. As the following chapter points out, these types of rent seeking or lobbying costs accompany legislative authority (at the federal level in the U.S.) over money held by the Social Security Trust Fund. When added to the costs related to reduced saving that we presented in Chapter 3, the total social harm caused by the U.S. Social Security system becomes even more substantial.

Notes to Chapter 4

1. Barro (1997) points out that academic economists (of the American Economic Association) have, by not restricting the output of newly minted economics PhDs over the years, been miserable at implementing monopoly restrictions. As he reports, a panel of Harvard economists voted the U.S. Postal Service as the best example of monopoly in America; coming in third is "almost any cable TV company" in America.

2. Interestingly, this is one area where academic research and journalism have intersected. Political commentators/writers have grasped and begun to use this aspect of the public choice tradition in their own analyses of political activity (see Will, 1992; Rauch, 1994). They often use the term "transfer seeking" instead of the term "rent seeking," however. Another relatively recent occurrence is

that a number of economics texts have been written with a major focus on public choice elements (see Ekelund and Tollison, 2000; Gwartney, Stroup, Sobel and Macpherson, 2003).

3. The traditional notion involves the "contrived scarcity" element in monopoly. That is, the monopoly restriction on output creates a deadweight loss in social welfare, given that the "unproduced" units have a marginal benefit to consumers which is less than their marginal opportunity cost in production. Therefore, the monopolist produces less than the *optimal* amount of output. The resulting loss in social welfare has been examined by many writers (Harberger, 1954; Schwartzman, 1960; Kamerschen, 1966; Worcester, 1973; Mixon and Ressler, 1998). These studies suggest that the traditional welfare loss to society due to monopoly restrictions ranges from about 0.08-percent of national income to about 8-percent of national income. According to Mixon and Ressler (1998: 24), this is equivalent to $5.8 to $580 billion each year (in 1995 dollars).

4. Some argue that monopolies have redeeming qualities. Schumpeter (1942), for instance, argues that monopolies are the engine of progress in a dynamic economy. Their profits are necessary for the research and development that leads to new innovations and technologies. This view, however, emphasizes their dynamic benefits; what remains is their static costs. Some argue for economic regulation of monopolies in order to minimize these static costs, however numerous studies have suggested that regulation often fails to restrict the price of the monopolized good to less-than monopoly levels (see Stigler, 1971; Stigler and Friedland, 1961; Peltzman, 1976; Caudill, Im and Kaserman, 1993; Jarrell, 1978; Moore, 1975; Upadhyaya, Raymond, and Mixon, 1997).

Other studies have suggested that, under regulation, the costs of production rise through expense preference behavior (see Mixon and Upadhyaya, 1999 and 2001). Brinig, Holcombe and Schwartzstein (1993) also point out that regulation of lobbyists generally serves the interests of those being lobbied (i.e., legislators), given that stringent regulation acts as a demand-revealing mechanism. That is, lobbying restrictions screen those interest groups that are willing to "pay" high prices for legislation/regulation or monopolistic restrictions from those less willing to "pay" high prices. This finding is not only consistent with the literature detailed above, it also fits nicely into the "market for laws" construct of Crain (1979) and Benson and Engin (1988).

5. Of course, this type of analysis applies to many other scenarios, such as competing resource investments by contestants to win The Miss America crown (e.g., they "invest" in beauty products, public relations consulting, speech and posture coaching, etc.), or competing resource investments to get a local liquor license or taxi cab medallion, both of which are often restricted by governments.

6. The scenario presented in the text and in Table 4.2 could be amended to fit the case of government transfers. For instance, the $2,000,000 figure might represent a line item in the federal budget, for each year of two years, whose present value is again $3,666,800 (at a 6% interest rate). The five competing groups for access to or use of this line item might be (1) the National Endowment for the Arts, (2) the Alabama Public Service Commission, (3) the University of California at Davis, (4) the Cincinnati Department of Parks and Recreation, and (5) the Florida Dairy Farmers Association. In this case, each group has the same expenditure rule, and rents (i.e., the line item amount itself)

will again be dissipated through these combined rent seeking expenditures (at least theoretically).

7.   The social opportunity costs of rent seeking in society can be enormous. Mixon and Wilkinson (2000a) examine how the macroeconomy of Japan has been significantly hampered by the development of a rent seeking society. The Mixon-Wilkinson study follows the Olson (1965, 1982, 1983, and 1988) tradition, positing that rent seeking organizations grow in size, scope and effectiveness as they age (or as society ages). Lastly, Mixon and Wilkinson (2000) also suggest, as does Sutter (1998), that rent seeking be mitigated constitutionally.

8.   In our hypothetical CATV monopoly (or federal budget line appropriation) story, the $3.7 million CATV profit (or budget line item) might be obtained from a rent seeking contest that produces an aggregate rent seeking cost equal to only a small fraction of the awarded amount (i.e., $3.7 million). In this view, the financial return to rent seeking effort is enormous. This is the type of outcome referred to by Tullock and other researchers looking into this issue. Most of these studies have compared measurable rent seeking costs, such as political campaign contributions, to the size of government (i.e., to government spending).

9.   One of the theories posited by Tullock (1989) in explaining the disparity between rent seeking costs and politically-directed transfers is that, perhaps, people view rent seeking (i.e., favor seeking) as immoral. Mixon and Wilkinson (2000b) explore this possibility by looking at rent seeking effort displayed (empirically) by tax-exempt, religious organizations. This study finds

that these organizations not only engage in rent seeking behavior, they often violate federal legal statutes in doing so.

10. Relating the empirical evidence to our hypothetical example might suggest that the CATV monopoly worth $3.7 million is awarded within a rent seeking contest that produces an aggregate rent seeking cost of, say, $1.5 million (these rent seeking costs might come in the form of direct and indirect political campaign support). In this case, government officials sold a prize worth $3.7 million for only $1.5 million (i.e., a $2.2 million disparity). These additional studies suggest, however, that other political favors were directed toward the government officials in position to award the CATV license. These include, but are not limited to, fancy restaurant dining, golf excursions, massage services, and promises of post-elective employment. These services, though largely unobserved, have a value that augments the direct, observed rent seeking costs measured by campaign support. In doing so, they reduce the $2.2 million disparity in our hypothetical scenario, and the real world disparity noted by Tullock (1980; 1989) and other researchers.

11. For a primer on public choice theory, see Tullock, Seldon, and Brady (2000). For excellent reviews of the rent seeking model in public choice, see Tollison (1982), Potters and Sloof (1996), and Jain (2001). Lastly, for a look at the added costs of "defensive rent seeking" and "rent defending," see McChesney (1987; 1991; 2001) and Mixon and Wilkinson (1999).

12. Mixon and Ressler (1998: 24) use a geometric approach to estimate that the sum of monetary and in-kind rent seeking costs associated with monopoly restrictions in the U.S. (in 1995 dollars) could be

as high as $1.2 trillion annually (a lower bound estimate, taken from a wide interval, for these costs is only about $12 billion/annually).

Chapter 5

Social Security Trust Fund Flows, Rent Seeking, and the Social Opportunity Costs of U.S. Public Policy

5.1. Introduction

This chapter complements Chapter 3 by exploring an additional social opportunity cost emanating from the institutional arrangements comprising the current U.S. Social Security System. Federal government budgetary authority over the Social Security Trust Fund, which holds the sum of excess contributions payments (and interest income) over benefits payments, provides elected legislators access to added federal tax dollars to fund budgetary items such as social programs, educational initiatives, national defense, and macroeconomic stimulus packages. With this budgetary authority comes the ability to re-distribute this wealth among interest groups in society. As the previous chapter points out, the now well known public choice theory of rent seeking suggests that efforts to influence the direction of public budgeting by coalitions is wasteful, in a normative sense, because the resources devoted to these income redistribution related activities could have been used more productively.

Data presented recently by Mixon (2002) are detailed in this chapter, suggesting that significant inflation-adjusted sums of money often flow into the coffers of the Social Security system's Trust Fund. In fact, from the 1985-1986 to the 1993-1994 Congressional cycles (i.e., the 99th U.S. Congress through the 103rd U.S. Congress), these *flows* ranged from a low of $17.34 billion (1985-1986) to a high of $66.14 billion (1991-1992) in *real* terms. These figures are quite substantial. To see just how substantial, recall that in early 1993, after just a few months in office and facing the remnants of an economic recession, then President Clinton called for a $19 billion (approximately) economic stimulus package in hopes of generating greater economic activity. This expenditure would have been about one-third of the money that *flowed into* the Social Security Trust Fund's account from the previous Congressional period (1991-1992). Additionally, Mississippi is currently requesting that the federal government live up to its obligation to provide federal funds to shore up its elections system in the wake of concerns emanating from the "aftermath of the 2000 presidential" election (The Editor, 2002). The positive Social Security Trust Fund flow from the 103rd Congress (1993-1994) alone could provide $381 million dollars to *each* of the 50 states for election systems reform, with the same sum (also available from that period's positive flow into the Fund) remaining for *each* state to make institutional changes in response to the aftermath of the 11 September 2001 terrorists attacks in New York, Washington, D.C., and Pennsylvania. Then, there are other popular sources of rent seeking in society, such as artists/entertainers who support a $100-$150 million annual budget line-item for funding of their activities. The money entering Social Security Trust Fund during 1993-1994 could provide this level of funding (in nominal terms) for over two centuries. The debate in the U.S. House over arts funding is often very heated; the relaxed budgetary constraint that results from maintaining control over the Social Security Trust Fund's coffers, wherein receipts do sometimes outweigh expenditures (over the year), quite likely lowers the contentiousness of these debates, however.

What follows in this chapter is a look at the empirical work in this area provided earlier by Mixon (2002). We will, however, offer new insights and some additional analysis that links the results presented in this section to the results presented in Chapter 3. Lastly, we will be able to provide a concise summary of the expansive social costs associated with U.S. public policy toward private saving (in the case of Social Security).

5.2. Rent Seeking and the Social Security Trust Fund: The Hypothesis

Over the past three decades, public choice economists have expanded the traditional notion of deadweight losses due to monopoly (as in Harberger, 1954) with the modern theory of rent seeking (see Chapter 4). This paradigm has expanded the notion of a monopoly loss to include competing resource investments to obtain monopoly profits. As Tullock (1989) has pointed out (see also Chapter 4), public choice economists have used government transfers more or less interchangeably with monopolistic restrictions through public franchising/licensing. As stated previously, the case for doing so is relatively straightforward. To a large extent, both are the result of rent seeking activity and normally involve large inefficiencies.[1] And, it is usually the case that most government transfers are not from the wealthy to the poor but from the poorly politically organized to the well politically organized (Mixon, 2002: 976).[2] Converting the formal analysis of rent seeking to deal with government transfers instead of monopolistic restrictions has been formally accomplished (see Tullock, 1970 and 1971).

Consistent with the rent seeking conversion above, recent studies have shown *positive* and *statistically significant* relationships between real government spending and overt levels of rent seeking effort, usually measured by campaign contributions (Mixon and Wilkinson, 1999; Lott, 2000). To examine the rent seeking model within the Social Security Trust Fund setting, a study by Mixon (2002) establishes the following statistical equation,

(5.1) CONT = α + (B•SENATE) + (Φ•PINC) + (γ•PREZ) + (Γ•CAND) + (Λ•PMAJ) + (δ •FICA) + ε,

where α, B, Φ, γ, Γ, Λ, and δ are parameters estimated by regression analysis. The dependent variable above (CONT) is equal to the *real* value of campaign contributions to all candidates running for U.S. House or U.S. Senate seats over each two-year election cycle from 1976-1994 (Mixon, 2002: 976). Therefore, the data set consists U.S. House observations and U.S. Senate observations over the 1976-1994 time frame denoted above. In this case, a panel data set is employed (see Baltagi, 2001).

SENATE (a dummy variable equal to 1 for Senate observations in the panel, and zero otherwise) is an important control variable given that each two-year election cycle consists of about 33 Senate races and 435 House races. It is generally more expensive to win a Senate seat; however, fewer Senate seats are up for grabs in a given election cycle. There are, therefore, competing cost considerations with the variable. It is likely, though, that the numerical effect (i.e., fewer seats up for election) dominates the cost-per-seat effect, and that SENATE will be negatively related to CONT (Mixon, 2002: 977).

CAND is the total number of candidates seeking office in either chamber of Congress (both in the primaries and general elections). It is expected to retain a positive relation to CONT, as is PINC, or the percentage of incumbents eligible for re-election that choose to seek re-election. The former expectation arises from the numerical effect of contested elections (in terms of the candidate count); the latter expectation arises because incumbents are successful at raising money and it will usually require larger monetary sums to unseat incumbents.[3] Next, PREZ is a dummy variable equal to one for Presidential election cycles, and zero otherwise. It is possible that contributors are more likely to give to congressional candidates during Presidential cycles in an attempt to usher in one-party government; conversely, midterm elections are notoriously volatile and could be driven by significantly larger campaign contributions or just create larger campaign contributions to combat the volatility.[4] Hence, no *a priori* expectation is posited here (Mixon, 2002: 977).

The size (in percentage terms) of the majority party may also play a role in determining the level of contributions to House and Senate candidates. For example, if a narrow majority exists in one branch, greater contributions might then be expected in an attempt to maintain or shift the balance of power in that branch. Therefore, one would expect Λ to retain a negative sign in equation (5.1) above. Lastly, the variable of interest in the Mixon (2002) study—FICA—measures the *real* value of net flows into the Social Security Trust Fund during each two-year election cycle by subtracting the two-year benefits payments from the two-year payroll tax receipts that fund the pension program. In this computation, only the OASDI (Old Age, Survivor and Disability Insurance) portion of the program is examined (Mixon, 2002: 977). Following the public choice model, as the size of government grows one expects greater levels of rent seeking activity. In this regard, Congress' budgetary authority over the balance of the Social Security Trust Fund would be an open door to special interest groups and coalitions seeking financial rewards from Congress. Therefore, one would expect that FICA and CONT will be positively related, *ceteris paribus*. In the next section, the estimation technique and statistical results are explored in detail.

5.3. Examining the Data on Social Security Trust Fund Flows

Following Greene (1997: 612-647) and Mixon (2002: 977), one can expect (1) that the variance will be quite different in the two time series (1976-1994), (2) the fates of the candidates for U.S. House and Senate seats, with regard to campaign contributions, will be tied to macroeconomic and legislative-chamber specific factors, leading to the correlation of disturbances across across congressional houses, and (3) that the errors are correlated over time. The Parks (1967) regression technique assumes heteroscedasticity, a first-order autoregressive structure, and contemporaneous correlation between the cross-sections. As Mixon (2002) points out, specifically the random errors, u_{it} (for i = 1, 2,..., N, and t = 1, 2,... T) have the structure:

(5.2) $E(u_{it}^2) = \sigma_{ii}$, $E(u_{it} u_{jt}) = \sigma_{ij}$ and $u_{it} = \rho_i u_{i, t-1} + \varepsilon_{it}$.

In this model the covariance matrix for the vector of random errors (u) can be expressed as V, which is estimated by a two-stage procedure, and β is then estimated by generalized least squares (GLS). The first step in estimating V involves the use of OLS to estimate β and obtain the fitted residuals ($\hat{u} = y - X\beta_{OLS}$). A consistent estimator of the first-order autoregressive parameter is obtained in the usual manner, and the autoregressive characteristic of the data is asymptotically removed by the transformation of taking weighted differences. The system is written as:

(5.3) $y*_{it} = \sum_{k=1}^{p} X*_{itk}\beta_k + u*_{it} (i = 1,2,...N; t = 1,2,...T)$

The second step in estimating the covariance matrix V is to apply OLS to the transformed model (obtaining $\hat{u}* = y* - X*\beta*_{OLS}$), from which the Parks estimator of σ_{ij} is calculated. The Parks estimator is unbiased, consistent and efficient. These properties will allow us to draw more definitive conclusions from the statistical estimations presented next.

The average election cycle contribution total over the period explored in Mixon (2002) is $185.43 million in *real* terms. On average, 87% of incumbents (in both branches of Congress) sought re-election throughout the 1976-1994 period, and about 1,007 candidates sought office (on average) across the two legislative branches. Lastly, the average size of the majority party across these two branches was 0.59 (or, 59%), while the average flow into the Social Security Trust Fund throughout this period was a sizable $17.26 billion in *real* terms.[5]

Table 5.1 presents regression results from an unrestricted version of equation (5.1) above.

Table 5.1
Summary of Parks Regression Estimates

Variable	Parks Estimator	*t*-value	Significance Level
constant	646.177	3.23	0.01
SENATE	-44.762	-1.32	>0.05
PINC	-124.403	-1.11	>0.05
PREZ	-12.328	-1.00	>0.05
CAND	0.037	2.38	0.05
PMAJ	-633.512	-3.40	0.01
FICA	0.001	3.68	0.01

Parks adjusted R^2 = 0.9088

Note: The dependent variable is, again CONT.
Source: Mixon (2002: 978).

Most of the Parks regression coefficients retain their expected signs, with CAND, PMAJ and FICA each achieving the 0.05 level of significance or better. The variable of interest, FICA, is attached to a Parks estimator (see δ from equation 5.1) whose value is 0.001, suggesting that the mean value of FICA (about $17 billion for the entire period) would generate rent seeking costs—associated with campaign contributions only—of about $17.3 million over a two-year election cycle, *ceteris paribus*. Though quite a significant sum, this figure remains remarkably below the theoretical expectation of public choice models (approximately $17 billion) and perpetuates Tullock's concern regarding the *observed* disparity in rent seeking costs and government transfers in the U.S. This point is made even further by Mixon (2002: 978). Table 5.2 below examines the level of rent seeking effort and the size of the return-to-effort ratio from the 99th through the 103rd Congress (i.e., 1985-86 through 1993-94). First, the (predicted) rent seeking costs

Table 5.2
Estimates of the Social Opportunity Costs of Rent Seeking Effort: The Case of the OASDI Trust Fund

Election Cycle	Rent Seeking Expectation (Theoretical)	Parks Model Estimate (Empirical)	Disparity (Approximate)
1985-1986	$17,335,770,000	$34,711,540	$17.3 billion
1987-1988	$31,868,130,000	$63,736,260	$31.8 billion
1989-1990	$64,192,810,000	$128,385,620	$64.1 billion
1991-1992	$66,143,980,000	$132,287,960	$66.0 billion
1993-1994	$38,124,160,000	$76,483,200	$38.1 billion

Sources: Mixon (2002: 978) and the Authors.

associated with efforts to influence expenditures of the Trust Fund are (predictably) quite sizable. They range from $34 million to $132 million per election cycle. However, the disparities (in returns and costs) are also all quite large; in effect, the predicted financial return to this *overt* rent seeking of the Social Security Trust Fund is on the order of $500 per $1 "invested" in the rent seeking effort. Of course, these figures certainly overestimate the return, given the in-kind rent seeking considerations discussed in the previous chapter, which (in sum) are likely to be substantial. It likely remains the case that the total social opportunity costs of this rent seeking—from both *overt* and *hidden, in-kind* efforts—are enormous.

5.4. *Closing Thoughts*

This chapter applies the concept of rent seeking and its social opportunity costs in the unique case of Social Security Trust Fund dollars. The *overt* rent seeking costs associated with use of the Trust Fund's resources are substantial. Those measured here—including only campaign contributions to candidates seeking U.S. House and Senate offices—range from about $35 million to $132 million (in *real* terms) during several recent Congressional cycles. When augmented by difficult-to-measure in-kind rent seeking efforts, these figures would likely grow significantly. The theoretical upper bound on the total social costs associated with this particular rent seeking effort, during the time period examined here, ranges from about $17 billion to $66 billion (in *real* terms) per Congressional election cycle.

In any scenario, these enormous costs supplement those detailed earlier in Chapter 3. The empirical evidence presented in Chapter 3 suggests that the current Social Security System reduces national saving, thus hindering capital formation in the macroeconomy and lowering the rate of economic growth. Additionally, the existence of Congressional budgetary over dollars that flow into the System's Trust Fund generates rent seeking costs that are also substantial. Given one of the findings presented in Chapter 3, that national saving is reduced by about 4.5-percent of national income due to the "substitution effect" inherent in Social Security wealth, the total cost of the public retirement program could easily be greater than 5-percent of national income when these rent seeking costs are included.

Notes to Chapter 5

1. Public choice scholars often refer to the rent seeking (and lobbying) costs within the political process as *government failure* (similar to the case where private market interactions sometimes produce *externalities*, suggesting the presence of *market failure*). Wittman (1995) argues, contrary to many public choice and political science models (e.g., Downs, 1957; Black, 1958; Hotelling, 1929; Bowen, 1943), that voters are fully informed and that government produces efficient results (i.e., there is no *government failure*). Boudreaux (1996: 117-118) offers the compelling argument, however, that tens of thousands of highly aggregated issues are on the table in each national election—from abortion to school choice to government provision of medical services to farm subsidies to child-welfare policies to tax rates—and that each voter (during a six year span) has a maximum of nine ballots to cast in four national elections. This suggests that political decisions by voters, as opposed to market decisions by consumers or households, are invariably cluttered with "romance pollution" (see also Brennan and Lomasky, 1993). Accordingly, these decisions are *un*informed, and contrary to Wittman (1995), are not likely to promote efficient policies or outcomes. The "romance pollution" referred to by Boudreaux (1996) emanates, in part, from the "expressiveness" often inherent in an individual's vote. For interesting empirical work on expressiveness in voting, see Copeland and Laband (2002).

2. See Will (1992) for an insightful look at the politics surrounding farm support (subsidy) programs in American during the 20th Century.

3. Recent studies suggest that incumbents are able to use C-SPAN and C-SPAN2 cameras as low-cost advertising media, thus making it even more important for challengers to visit the hustings (Crain and Goff, 1988; Greene, 1992; Mixon, Hobson and Upadhyaya, 2001; Mixon, 2001 and 2002; Mixon and Upadhyaya, 2002; Mixon, Gibson, and Upadhyaya, 2003).

4. A recent example of this volatility occurred in the 1994 U.S. House elections, wherein the Republicans took control of the House (in a big swing) for the first time in decades.

5. Exactly one-half of these election cycles were midterm cycles, and one-half of the panel is represented by observations drawn on each branch of Congress (Mixon, 2002: 976).

Chapter 6

Social Security, Private Saving, and Social Opportunity Costs: An Appraisal

In the preceding chapters we have built the case that the current U.S. Social Security system causes two socially costly outcomes: it reduces national savings, perhaps by as much as 50-percent from its potential, and it directs a significant flow of resources, through Congress' budgetary authority over the system's Trust Fund, into an already growing rent seeking environment in Washington, D.C. These costs are substantial. Table 6.1 below summarizes some of the results presented in Table 3.14 (see Chapter 3) and Table 5.2 (see Chapter 5) above. It

Table 6.1
Social Opportunity Costs and Social Security: The Estimates

	Loss in National Saving	Rent Seeking Costs
Lower Bound	$96 billion [without taxes] (1976 dollars)	$18 million [without *in-kind* efforts] (1982/84 dollars)

64

Upper Bound	$128 billion [without taxes] (1976 dollars)	$66 million [without *in-kind* efforts] (1982/84 dollars)
Lower Bound	$119 billion [with taxes] (1976 dollars)	$9 billion [with *in-kind* efforts] (1982/84 dollars)
Upper Bound	$154 billion [with taxes] (1976 dollars)	$33 billion [with *in-kind* efforts] (1982/84 dollars)

Note: The figures above represent annual costs.

points out that even the lower bound estimates for the reduction in savings ($96 billion) and rent seeking costs ($18 million) per year are quite sizable. When the upper bound estimates are considered, the latter of these costs grows exponentially. In this case, the reduction in savings is equal to $154 billion, while the rent seeking costs rise to about $33 billion. Of course, these comparisons are not as informative as they could perhaps be, given that the dollar figures in each category represent different purchasing powers (i.e., different time periods). We sought to strengthen this comparison with an additional summary, which is contained in Table 6.2 below.

Table 6.2
Social Opportunity Costs and Social Security: Further Examination

	Loss in National Saving	*Rent Seeking Costs*
Lower Bound	$281 billion [without taxes] (1998 dollars)	$30 million [without *in-kind* efforts] (1998 dollars)

Upper Bound	$375 billion [without taxes] (1998 dollars)	$110 million [without *in-kind* efforts] (1998 dollars)
Lower Bound	$349 billion [with taxes] (1998 dollars)	$15 billion [with *in-kind* efforts] (1998 dollars)
Upper Bound	$451 billion [with taxes] (1998 dollars)	$55 billion [with *in-kind* efforts] (1998 dollars)

Note: The figures above represent annual costs.
Source: *The Statistical Abstract of the United States 1999*, Washington, D.C., U.S. Bureau of the Census.

Here, all of the data are converted to 1998 dollars, yielding more comparable figures. Expectedly, the reductions in saving due to the presence of Social Security Wealth are much larger than the associated rent seeking costs due to lobbying the U.S. Congress for access to Trust Fund (dollar) flows. An upper bound (lower bound) estimate on the former is $451 billion ($281 billion) per year; for the latter, the figure is $55 billion ($30 million) per year. Again, differences in upper (lower) bound estimates exist within the two categories, depending upon the inclusion or exclusion of payroll taxes and *in-kind* rent seeking efforts. When both are included, and the figures are summed together, the upper (lower) bound estimate on the reduction in savings and rent seeking costs associated with Social Security Wealth reach an astounding $506 billion ($364 billion), in 1998 dollars. These figures certainly strengthen the case for reform of the current system.

The current Social Security debate in America usually centers, however, on comparisons of the financial returns earned from the current Social Security system with those potentially earned by private alternatives. In the story we told in Chapter 1, the return to a moderately conservative private portfolio was 4.89-percent, while the yield on the Social Security plan is negative (-0.72-percent). These numbers clearly indicate why the emphasis is often placed on comparing the financial returns, and why many young Americans favor a private option.

What may not be evident, though, is that some of the costs detailed in this volume could be avoided through privatization of the system. Privatization, coupled with a removal of Congressional budgetary authority over workers' retirement contributions, would prevent Senators and Representatives from dipping into the Fund (as they do now) to provide special interest spending of all sorts. As we pointed out above, privatization of this sort would, perhaps, reduce the size of the rent seeking industry in Washington, D.C. by as much as $55 billion annually in real terms (using recent data). Privatization of system, whereby American workers redirected their payroll taxes into higher yielding portfolio options (as in the story we told in Chapter 1), would also likely provide significantly greater amounts of American savings to private businesses, which could be used to expand the nation's productive capacity and provide for higher standards of living in the future.

Chapter 7

Public Policy and Saving: Other Avenues for Debate

7.1. Introduction

In this study we have, so far, concentrated on the social costs of American public policy toward national saving, specifically with regard to the U.S. Social Security system. Although we have brought to the forefront some new concerns to this *general* policy debate through our exploration focused on Social Security—namely, that there are substantial rent seeking costs associated with lobbying effort to influence the distribution of Social Security Trust Fund flows, the political/academic debate concerning federal budgetary policy and private saving and investment is not new. For instance, the relationship between government deficits and national saving and investment in the U.S. has wide-ranging and substantial implications. As Pradhan and Upadhyaya (2001: 1,745) point out, the empirical literature in this area can be broadly classified into two categories: the first condemns deficit-spending (with regard to saving and investment), while the second supports deficit-spending. This chapter will take a brief look at this debate, paying special attention to results from a recent study on this issue (Pradhan and Upadhyaya, 2001).

7.2. Federal Government Budget Deficits, National Saving, and Investment: New Evidence

As Pradhan and Upadhyaya (2001: 1,745) point out, the conventional position on budget deficits is that they lower investment and increase trade deficits in a macroeconomy. A common explanation for this is that deficits drive up real interest rates and "crowd out" domestic investment, thus reducing economic growth, *ceteris paribus.* "The amount of crowding out depends on the degree to which higher domestic interest rates attract foreign investment. To the extent that the debt-induced increase in the interest rate leads to an inflow of capital from abroad, the domestic currency appreciates and crowds out net exports rather than domestic investment. Most economists believe that in the long run, budget deficits reduce [the] capital stock,…and place a burden on future generations. While living standards are higher in the present [period], they will be lower in the future (Pradhan and Upadhyaya, 2001: 1,745)."

There are at least two positions against the view described above. One of these is held by Eisner and Piper (1984) and Eisner (1986), who contend that the federal budget deficit is overstated for two main reasons: inflation tends to raise measured deficits, and federal deficits are overstated in national income accounts because a sizable part of the government's spending is actually *investment,* and therefore should not be counted as current expenditure.[1]

In a recent paper, Eisner (1994) shows, using data from 1972-1991, that real budget deficits have increased national saving. He argues that this effect on national saving is consistent with the hypothesis that federal deficits can increase national saving by stimulating more employment and investment (through a Keynesian expansion). However, as Pradhan and Upadhyaya (2001) point out, a number of additional factors that affect saving in the macroeconomy are omitted in Eisner's analysis. It is possible, for instance, that an actual reduction in national saving could have been more than offset by demographic changes. The working-age population grew steadily from the 1960s to the 1980s as baby boomers reached adulthood. Such a demographic shift, for instance, can "be expected to have a positive effect on national saving (Pradhan and Upadhyaya, 2001: 1,746)."

The Pradhan-Upadhyaya (2001) study examines the relationship between budget deficits and national saving using annual data from 1967 to 1996, and it also accounts for the aforementioned omitted factors. Their model examines, as the dependent variable, two different measures of national saving over time. These are (1) the difference between national income and the sum of private and government consumption, and (2) the sum of gross private domestic investment (domestic saving) and net foreign receipts (foreign saving). These variables are then combined with the real exchange rate, defined as the multilateral trade-weighted value of the U.S. dollar adjusted by the CPI and the foreign price index, and the real interest rate, defined as the nominal interest rate minus the inflation rate. A demographic variable is included, and defined as the portion of the working-age population to total population (ages 15-65).

Other variables include the money supply (measured as a percent of GDP), and the variable of interest, the federal deficit (measured as a percent of GDP).[2] After establishing the stationarity of the data/variable series using Augmented Dickey-Fuller and Phillips-Perron unit root procedures (see Chapter 3 above), a Johansen's cointegration test indicates the existence of at least one cointegrating vector, and thus a long run relationship among the variables (see Chapter 3 above). Table 7.1 below presents the estimates of the cointegrated vectors normalized on national saving.

Table 7.1
Cointegrated Vector Normalized on National Saving

Variable	Estimated Parameters	
	(on NS1)	(on NS2)
budget deficits	-0.01	-1.34
money supply	-0.38	-0.54
real exchange rate	0.0002	0.0009
real interest rate	-0.005	-0.011
working-age population	0.458	1.610

Note: NS1 and NS2 represent the two separate measures of saving described in the text.
Source: Pradhan and Upadhyaya (2001).

These cointegrating vectors represent "the long run response of the dependent variable [national saving] to some change in the explanatory variables (Pradhan and Upadhyaya, 2001: 1,748)." Interestingly, the long run response of national saving to budget deficits is negative.

Pradhan and Upadhyaya (2001) present parameter estimates from an error-correction model yielding several conclusions. These are included in Table 7.2 below. Among these is evidence

Table 7.2

An Error-Correction Model of National Saving, 1967-1996

Variable	ΔNS1	ΔNS2
constant	-0.003	-0.002
Δdeficit	-0.405*	-0.254
Δdeficit lag	-0.147	0.283
Δmoney supply	0.182	-0.310**
Δmoney supply lag	0.037	0.062
Δreal exchange rate	0.0002	8.13e-5
Δreal exhange rate lag	-9.84e-5	0.0002
Δreal interest rate	0.004**	0.003**
Δreal interest rate lag	0.002	0.0001
Δworking-age pop.	1.016***	0.859*
error correction term	-0.818***	-0.624***
adjusted R-square	0.625	0.555
D.W.	2.420	1.956
F-statistic	5.325***	4.237***
RESET F-statistic	0.882	0.262

Note: ***(**)[*] denotes the 0.01(0.05)[0.10] level of significance.
Source: Pradhan and Upadhyaya (2001: 1,749).

suggesting that federal government budget deficits are significantly *inversely* related to national saving (NS1) over time. As they state,

"…the contemporaneous effect of budget deficits on national saving is negative and statistically significant with NS1. In the case of NS2, even though it is not significant at the conventional level it still carries an appropriate sign and the size of the coefficient is quite large…This finding is contradictory to the findings of Eisner (1994) and suggests that budget deficits, in fact, could have negatively affected national saving [in the U.S.]" (Pradhan and Upadhyaya, 2001: 1,749)

Furthermore, increases in the working-age population (ratio), an omitted factor in Eisner's analysis, also significantly increase the level of national saving in the macroeconomy. The fact that their regression specification withstands a regression specification error test is also encouraging.

7.3. Closing Comments

This chapter addresses a separate element—unrelated to the U.S. Social Security system—in the ongoing debate concerning the relationship between public policy and national saving. If the Pradhan and Upadhyaya (2001) results are robust, as they appear to be, the relationship between federal government budget deficits and national saving in the U.S. is, at best, nonexistent. In a worst case scenario, their relationship is significantly negative. In this case, the losses to national saving detailed in Chapter 3 above are further augmented. It could, therefore, be the case that the reduction in national saving from the combined impact of Social Security *and* federal deficits in the 1980s reached perhaps as high as 70-percent of potential total private saving. With deficits again looming over the horizon, these combined costs deserve more consideration in the future.

Notes to Chapter 7

1. While Eisner argues that these adjustments to the national income accounts matter, Gramlich (1984) shows that these corrections make little difference in assessing U.S. fiscal history. For a look at

the second type of defense of budget deficits—which is based on Ricardian equivalence—see Barro (1974).

2. See Pradhan and Upadhyaya (2001: 1,746-1,747) for a lengthy and detailed discussion regarding the expected relationships between the regressors and national saving (the dependent variable).

Bibliography

Alesina, A. and L.H. Summers (1993) "Central bank independence and macroeconomic performance: Some comparative evidence," *Journal of Money, Credit, and Banking* 25: 151-162.

Alesina, A., N. Roubini, with G.D. Cohen (1997) *Political cycles and the macroeconomy*, Cambridge, MA: The MIT Press.

Ando, A. and F. Modigliani (1963) "The 'life cycle' hypothesis of saving: Aggregate implications and tests," *American Economic Review* 53: 55-84.

Baltagi, B.H. (2001) *Econometric analysis of panel data*, New York, NY: John Wiley & Sons, Inc.

Barro, R.J. (1974) "Are government bonds new wealth?" *Journal of Political Economy* 82: 1,095-1,117.

Barro, R.J. (1997) *Getting it right: Markets and choices in a free society*, Cambridge, MA: The MIT Press.

Barro, R.J. (1999) *Determinants of economic growth: A cross-country empirical study*, Cambridge, MA: The MIT Press.

Benson, B.L. and E.M. Engin (1988) "The market for laws: An economic analysis of legislation," *Southern Economic Journal* 54: 732-745.

Black, D. (1958) *The theory of committees and elections*, Cambridge, MA: Cambridge University Press.

Boudreaux, D.J. (1996) "Was your high school civics teacher right after all?" *The Independent Review* 1: 111-128.

Bowen, H.R. (1943) "The interpretation of voting in the allocation of economic resources," *Quarterly Journal of Economics* 58: 27-48.

Brennan, G. and L. Lomasky (1993) *Democracy and decision*, New York, NY: Cambridge University Press.

Brinig, M.F., R.G. Holcombe, and L. Schwartzstein (1993) "The regulation of lobbyists," *Public Choice* 77: 377-384.

Buchanan, J.M. and G. Tullock (1962) *The calculus of consent*, Ann Arbor, MI: University of Michigan Press.

The Editor (2002) "State needs funding from U.S. Congress," *The Hattiesburg American* (10 August): 7A.

Caudill, S.B., B.G. Im, and D.L. Kaserman (1993) "Modeling regulatory behavior: The economic theory of regulation versus alternative theories and simple rules of thumb," *Journal of Regulatory Economics* 5: 251-262.

Copeland, C. and D.N. Laband (2002) "Expressiveness and voting," *Public Choice* 110: 351-363.

Crain, W.M. (1979) "Cost and output in the legislative firm," *The Journal of Legal Studies* 8: 607-621.

Crain, W.M. and B.L. Goff (1988) *Televised legislatures: Political infor-mation technology and public choice*, Boston, MA: Kluwer Academic Publishers.

Cukierman, A. (1992) *Central bank strategy, credibility, and independence*, Cambridge, MA: The MIT Press.

Dascher, K. (2000) "Are politics and geography related? Evidence from a cross-section of capital cities," *Public Choice* 105: 373-392.

Downs, A. (1957) *An economic theory of democracy*, New York, NY: Harper & Row.

Eisner, R. and P. Piper (1984) "A new view of the federal debt and budget deficits," *American Economic Review* 74: 11-29.

Eisner, R. (1986) *How real is the federal deficit?* New York, NY: The Free Press.

Eisner, R. (1994) "National saving and budget deficits," *Review of Economics and Statistics* 76: 181-186.

Ekelund, R.B., Jr. and R.D. Tollison (2000) *Economics: Private markets and public choice*, Reading, MA: Addison-Wesley.

Elder, J. and P. Kennedy (2001) "Testing for unit roots: What should students be taught?" *Journal of Economic Education* 32: 137-146.

Enders, W. (1995) *Applied econometric time series*, New York, NY: John Wiley & Sons, Inc.

Engle, R.F. and C.W.J. Granger (1987) "Cointegration and error-correction: Representation, estimation and testing," *Econometrica* 55: 251-276.

Feldstein, M.S. (1974) "Social security, induced retirement, and aggregate capital accumulation," *Journal of Political Economy* 82: 905-926.

Feldstein, M.S. (1982) "Social security and private saving: Reply," *Journal of Political Economy* 90: 630-642.

Feldstein, M.S. (1995) "Would privatizing social security raise economic welfare?" National Bureau of Economic Research Working Paper No. 5281.

Feldstein, M.S. (1996) "Social security and saving: New time series estimates," *National Tax Journal* 49: 151-164.

Gibson, M.T. (2003) "Future employment promises as rent-seeking in representative government," *International Journal of Social Economics*, forthcoming.

Gramlich, E. (1984) "How bad are the large deficits?" in G. Mills and T. Palmer, *Federal budget policy in the 1980s*, Washington, D.C.: The Urban Institute.

Greene, K.V. (1992) "The nature of political services, legislative turnover, and television," *Public Choice* 70: 267-276.

Greene, W.H. (1997) *Econometric analysis*, Upper Saddle River, NJ: Prentice Hall.

Grier, K. and M.C. Munger (1991) "Committee assignments, constituent preferences, and campaign contributions," *Economic Inquiry* 29: 24-43.

Gwartney, J.D., R.L. Stroup, R.S. Sobel and D.A. Macpherson (2003) *Economics: Private & public choice*, Mason, OH: South-Western.

Harberger, A.O. (1954) "Monopoly and resource allocation," *American Economic Review* 44: 77-87.

Havrilesky, T. (1995) *The pressures on American monetary policy*, Boston, MA: Kluwer Academic Publishers.

Hotelling, H. (1929) "Stability in competition," *The Economic Journal* 39: 41-57.

Hubbard, R.G. (2000) *Money, the financial system, and the economy*, Reading, MA: Addison-Wesley.

Hutchinson, H.D. (1992) *Money, banking, and the U.S. economy,* Englewood Cliffs, NJ: Prentice Hall.

Jain, A.K. (2001) "Corruption: A review," *Journal of Economic Surveys* 15: 71-121.

Jarrell, G.A. (1978) "The demand for state regulation of the electric utility industry," *Journal of Law and Economics* 21: 269-295.

Johansen, S. (1988) "Structural analysis of cointegration vectors," *Journal of Economic Dynamics and Control* 12: 231-254.

Johansen, S. and K. Juselius (1990) "Maximum likelihood estimation and inference on cointegration—with application to the demand for money," *Oxford Bulletin of Economics and Statistics* 52: 169-210.

Kamerschen, D. (1966) "An estimation of the welfare losses from monopoly in the American economy," *Western Economic Journal* 4: 221-236.

Kennedy, P. (1998) *A guide to econometrics,* Cambridge, MA: The MIT Press.

Krueger, A.O. (1974) "The political economy of the rent seeking society," *American Economic Review* 64: 291-303.

Laband, D.N. and J.P. Sophocleus (1991) "The social costs of rent seeking: First estimates," *Public Choice* 58: 269-275.

Laband, D.N. (1991) Review of G. Tullock's, *The economics of special privilege and rent seeking* in *Public Choice* 72: 241-243.

Laband, D.N. and J.P. Sophocleus (1992) "An estimate of resource expenditures on transfer activity in the United States," *Quarterly Journal of Economics* 107: 959-983.

Laband, D.N. and G.C. McClintock (2001) *The transfer society*, Washington, D.C.: The Cato Institute.

Leamer, E.E. (1978) *Specification searches: Ad hoc inference with nonexperimental data*, New York, NY: John Wiley.

Leimer, D.R. and S.D. Lesnoy (1982) "Social security and private saving: New time series evidence," *Journal of Political Economy* 90: 606-629.

Lipford, J.W. (2001) "How transparent is the U.S. budget?" *The Independent Review* 5: 575-591.

Lott, J.R., Jr. (2000) "A simple explanation for why campaign expenditures are increasing: Government is getting bigger," *Journal of Law and Economics* 43: 359-394.

McChesney, F.S. (1987) "Rent extraction and rent creation in the economic theory of regulation," *The Journal of Legal Studies* 16: 101-118.

McChesney, F.S. (1991) "Rent extraction and interest-group organization in a Coasian model of regulation," *The Journal of Legal Studies* 20: 73-90.

McChesney, F.S. (2001) "Rent seeking and rent extraction," in *The Elgar Companion to Public Choice*. edited by William F. Shughart, II and Laura Razzolini, Cheltenham, U.K.: Edward Elgar.

Mitchell, O.S. and S.P. Zeldes (1996) "Social security privatization: A structure for analysis," *American Economic Review* 86: 363-367.

Mixon, F.G., Jr., D.N. Laband, and R.B. Ekelund, Jr. (1994) "Rent seeking and hidden in-kind resource distortion: Some empirical evidence," *Public Choice* 78: 171-185.

Mixon, F.G., Jr. (1995) "To the Capitol, Driver: Limousine services as a rent seeking device in state capital cities," *Rivista Internazionale di Scienze Economiche e Commerciali* 42: 663-670.

Mixon, F.G., Jr. and R.W. McKenzie (1996) "Learning to rent-seek: Collective action and in-kind benefits in the public sector," *Applied Economics Letters* 3: 755-757.

Mixon, F.G., Jr. and J.A. Ladner (1998) "Sending federal fiscal power back to the states: Federal block grants and the value of state legislative offices," *Journal of Public Finance and Public Choice* 16: 27-41.

Mixon, F.G., Jr. and R.W. Ressler (1998) "Integrating the concept of rent seeking into the economics principles classroom: Evidence from survey data," *Journal of Education for Business* 74: 24-27.

Mixon, F.G., Jr. and K.P. Upadhyaya (1999) "The impact of economic regulation on attempts to curb expense preference behavior: A micro-data analysis of CEO compensation schemes for electric utilities," *Energy Economics* 21: 185-194.

Mixon, F.G., Jr. and J.B. Wilkinson (1999) "Maintaining the status quo: Federal government budget deficits and defensive rent seeking," *Journal of Economic Studies* 26: 5-14.

Mixon, F.G., Jr., M.T. Gibson, and K.P. Upadhyaya (2000) "Regulation, labor costs and employment in the U.S. Congress," *Journal of Public Finance and Public Choice* 18: 59-70.

Mixon, F.G., Jr. and J.B. Wilkinson (2000a) "Codifying the principles of a welfare state: An analysis of 'MacArthur's Constitution' for Japan," *International Journal of Social Economics* 27: 272-285.

Mixon, F.G., Jr. and J.B. Wilkinson (2000b) "Is rent-seeking immoral? Examining the behavior of religion-based political action committees and coalitions," *Applied Economics Letters* 7: 467-473.

Mixon, F.G., Jr. (2001) "A discrete-time hazard model of the adoption of legislative television: Evidence from the U.S. Congress, 1961-1986," *Applied Economics* 33: 1,881-1,887.

Mixon, F.G., Jr., D.L. Hobson, and K.P. Upadhyaya (2001) "Gavel-to-gavel congressional television coverage as political advertising: The impact of C-SPAN on legislative sessions," *Economic Inquiry* 39: 351-364.

Mixon, F.G., Jr. and K.P. Upadhyaya (2001) "Curbing expense preference behavior in commercial banking: Econometric evidence," *Applied Financial Economics* 11: 613-617.

Mixon, F.G., Jr. (2002) "Social security trust fund flows and the welfare costs of rent seeking," *Applied Economics* 34: 975-979.

Mixon, F.G., Jr. (2002) "Does legislative television alter the relationship between voters and politicians?" *Rationality and Society* 14: 109-128.

Mixon, F.G., Jr., W.C. Sawyer and K.P. Upadhyaya (2002) "Unit root test popularity among economists: Sampling the literature," *Economia Internazionale* 55: 37-45.

Mixon, F.G., Jr. and K.P. Upadhyaya (2002) "Legislative television as an institutional entry barrier: The impact of C-SPAN2 on turnover in the U.S. Senate, 1946-1998," *Public Choice*, forthcoming.

Mixon, F.G., Jr., M.T. Gibson, and K.P. Upadhyaya (2003) "Has legislative television changed legislator behavior? C-SPAN2 and the frequency of Senate filibustering," *Public Choice*, forthcoming.

Moore, C.G. (1975) "Has electricity regulation resulted in higher prices? An econometric evaluation utilizing a calibrated regulatory input variable," *Economic Inquiry* 7: 207-220.

Nelson, C.R. and C.I. Plosser (1982) "Trends and random walks in macroeconomic time series," *Journal of Monetary Economics* 10: 139-162.

Olson, M. (1965) *The logic of collective action: Public goods and the theory of groups*, Cambridge, MA: Harvard University Press.

Olson, M. (1982) *The rise and decline of nations*, New Haven, CT: Yale University Press.

Olson, M. (1983) "The South will fall again: The South as leader and laggard in economic growth," *Southern Economic Journal* 49: 917-932.

Olson, M. (1988) "The productivity slowdown, the oil shocks, and the real cycle," *Journal of Economic Perspectives* 2: 43-69.

Parks, R.W. (1967) "Efficient estimation of a system of regression equations when disturbances are both serially correlated and contemporaneously correlated," *Journal of the American Statistical Association* 62: 500-509.

Peltzman, S. (1976) "Toward a more general theory of regulation," *Journal of Law and Economics* 19: 211-240.

Phillips, P.C.B. (1987) "Time series regression with unit roots," *Econometrica* 55: 277-301.

Phillips, P.C.B. and P. Perron (1988) "Testing for a unit root in time series regression," *Biometrica* 75: 335-346.

Posner, R.A. (1975) "The social costs of monopoly and regulation," *Journal of Political Economy* 83: 43-69.

Potters, J. and R. Sloof (1996) "Interest groups: A survey of empirical models that try to assess their influence," *European Journal of Political Economy* 12: 403-442.

Pradhan, G. and K.P. Upadhyaya (2001) "The impact of budget deficits on national saving in the USA," *Applied Economics* 33: 1,745-1,750.

Rauch, J. (1994) *Demosclerosis: The silent killer of American government*, New York, NY: Times Books.

Snyder, J.M., Jr. (1990) "Campaign contributions as investments: The U.S. House of Representatives, 1980-1986," *Journal of Political Economy* 98: 1,095-1,127.

Snyder, J.M., Jr. (1993) "The market for campaign contributions: Evidence from the U.S. Senate, 1980-1986," *Economics and Politics* 5: 219-240.

Sobel, R.S. and T.A. Garrett (2002) "On the measurement of rent seeking and its social opportunity cost," *Public Choice* 112: 115-136.

Schumpeter, J. A. (1942) *Capitalism, socialism, and democracy*, New York, NY: Harper & Row.

Schwartzman, D. (1960) "The burden of monopoly," *Journal of Political Economy* 58: 627-630.

Sollars, D. (1996) "Rent seeking in state capitals, 1950-1990," Unpublished Manuscript, Auburn University at Montgomery.

Stigler G.J. and C. Friedland (1962) "What can regulators regulate? The case of electricity," *Journal of Law and Economics* 5: 1-16.

Stigler, G.J. (1971) "The theory of economic regulation," *Bell Journal of Economics and Management Science* 2: 3-21.

Stratmann, T. (1991) "What do campaign contributions buy? Deciphering causal effects of money and votes," *Southern Economic Journal* 57: 606-620.

Stratmann, T. (1995) "Campaign contributions and congressional voting: Does the timing of contributions matter?" *Review of Economics and Statistics* 77: 127-136.

Sutter, D. (1995) "Constitutional politics within the interest group model," *Constitutional Political Economy* 6: 127-137.

Sutter, D. (1998) "Constitutions and the growth of government," *Journal of Economic Behavior and Organization* 34: 129-142.

Tollison, R.D. (1982) "Rent seeking: A survey," *Kyklos* 35: 575-602.

Tullock, G. (1959) "Problems of majority voting," *Journal of Political Economy* 67: 571-579.

Tullock, G. (1967) "The welfare costs of tariffs, monopolies and theft," *Western Economic Journal* 5: 224-232.

Tullock, G. (1970) "Simple algebraic logrolling model," *American Economic Review* 60: 419-426.

Tullock, G. (1971) "The cost of transfers," *Kyklos* 24: 629-643.

Tullock, G. (1980) "Efficicient rent seeking," in J.M. Buchanan, R.D. Tollison, and G. Tullock (eds.) *Toward a theory of the rent seeking society*, College Station, TX: Texas A&M Press.

Tullock, G. (1989) *The economics of special privilege and rent seeking*, Boston, MA: Kluwer Academic Publishing.

Tullock, G. (1997) "Where's the rectangle?" *Public Choice* 91: 149-159.

Tullock, G. (1998) "Which rectangle?" *Public Choice* 96: 405-410.

Tullock, G., A. Seldon and G. L. Brady (2000) *Government: Whose obedient servant? A primer in public choice*, London: The Institute of Economic Affairs.

Upadhyaya, K.P., J.E. Raymond, and F.G. Mixon, Jr. (1997) "The economic theory of regulation versus alternative theories for the electric utilities industry: A simultaneous probit model," *Resource and Energy Economics* 19: 191-202.

Will, G. (1992) *Restoration: Congress, term limits and the recovery of deliberative democracy*, New York, NY: The Free Press.

Wittman, D. (1995) *The myth of democratic failure*, Chicago, IL: University of Chicago Press.

Worcester, D. (1973) "New estimates of the welfare loss to monopoly in the United States, 1956-1969," *Southern Economic Journal* 40: 234-245.

The Authors

Franklin G. Mixon, Jr. is the Business Advisory Council Professor of Economics at The University of Southern Mississippi. He received his PhD in economics from Auburn University in 1992, and has also held a faculty post at Southeastern Louisiana University. His research interests include the economic modeling of the political process, and industrial organization. His work has been published in numerous scholarly journals, with recent pieces being published by *Economics of Governance*, *Journal of Money, Credit, and Banking*, *Public Choice*, *Rationality and Society*, and *Economic Inquiry*. He is currently serving on the editorial boards of the *International Journal of Business and Economics* and the *Journal of Economics and Finance Education*.

Kamal P. Upadhyaya is an Associate Professor of Economics at the University of New Haven. He received his PhD in economics from Auburn University, and he has also held faculty positions at Salisbury State University and Pennsylvania State University. His research examines international trade, macroeconomics, and economic development issues, and it has recently been published by *Economic Inquiry*, *Public Choice*, *Journal of Development Studies*, *Economics Letters*, and the *International Trade Journal*.

www.ingramcontent.com/pod-product-compliance
Lightning Source LLC
Chambersburg PA
CBHW021544200526
45163CB00015B/1544